Does School Choice Work? Effects on Student Integration and Achievement

• • •

Julian R. Betts
Lorien A. Rice
Andrew C. Zau
Y. Emily Tang
Cory R. Koedel

2006

Library of Congress Cataloging-in-Publication Data

Does school choice work? : effects on student integration and achievement /
Julian R. Betts ... [et al.].

p. cm.

ISBN-13: 978-1-58213-114-6

ISBN-10: 1-58213-114-7

1. School choice—California—San Diego. 2. Public schools—California—San Diego. 3. School integration—California—San Diego. 4. Academic achievement—California—San Diego. I. Betts, Julian R.

LB1027.9.D63 2006

379.1'110973—dc22

2006023825

Foreword

To even the most informed parents, tracking the evolution of school reform can be a daunting task. There is plenty of public information on the poor test performance of many of our nation's children. There is much less systematic information on what is being done about it and which programs have the greatest chance of success. Reform programs are numerous, ranging from test-based accountability to putting mayors in charge of school systems. Some examine how schools are organized and focus on best practices, tracking, class size, and "whole-school" reform. Others stress the importance of teaching and learning through improved math instruction, English-language learning, and the design of professional development. Families with children in our public schools might well experience one or more of these and other reform efforts and reasonably ask: "Are any of these programs making a difference?"

More assessments of school reform are under way today than perhaps ever before in the history of American education. And most of these assessments are trying to answer that very question. This PPIC report, *Does School Choice Work? Effects on Student Integration and Achievement,* answers that question for a category of school reform programs known as school choice. School choice allows the parent and student to select a school other than the one in their immediate neighborhood. It is argued that choice gives students in below-average schools a chance to attend better schools, thus improving their achievement. A second argument is that once students begin to "vote with their feet," school principals will want to compete for the best students and therefore have incentives to provide the best possible education to the student "consumer."

In the early 2000s in the San Diego Unified School District, 28 percent of students chose alternative schools. Because of an extensive database compiled by SDUSD in cooperation with PPIC, the authors were in a unique position to find out who chose to attend an alternative school and whether that choice made any difference in academic achievement. The findings are striking. Black students were twice as likely as others to apply for an alternative school under one of four programs. And test scores were not the primary factor in influencing the decision to try an alternative school. Overall, the choice programs in San Diego are increasing the integration of whites and nonwhites, and decreasing very mildly the integration of students with low and high test scores.

The second major conclusion is that on the whole there was no systemic improvement or deterioration in test scores from participating in a choice program. There were some exceptions to this, but it is clear that school choice did not improve student performance in quite the way its proponents had hoped. Nevertheless, the authors conclude that high academic achievement may not be the sole criterion for the "good" school parents want their children to attend. Physical safety and generally higher socioeconomic settings might have also played a part in the decision—or else parents may have simply overestimated the benefits of a new school on their child's academic achievements.

These findings from SDUSD are important for other districts in California and for the nation as a whole. First, the data are collected in a way that makes them some of the best for analyzing the tough question: "Did it make a difference?" Second, the federal No Child Left Behind law requires that students at schools judged to be failing be provided district-funded busing to another school. At a minimum, the results from San Diego raise doubts about the ability of choice programs alone to increase the achievement of participants. They also suggest that parents and students may be expecting more from an improved public education system than higher test scores. Whatever the implications for No Child Left Behind and for other pressures to move toward choice, there is now a solid set of findings on one of the most dramatic school choice experiences in the United States, and the watchword should be: "Proceed with caution."

David W. Lyon
President and CEO
Public Policy Institute of California

Summary

School choice refers to the various ways parents can choose a school for their children. Throughout U.S. history, parents have been able to choose among schools indirectly by choosing where to live. But today, many other avenues are also available. For instance, many districts offer open-enrollment programs, busing and magnet school programs, charter schools, and, in a few cases, vouchers that allow some families to send their children to private schools.

Throughout its long and varied history, school choice has been a controversial topic in American politics. Proponents argue that more affluent families have long enjoyed school choice, through both private schools and the ability to move to better schools by buying a house in the school's attendance area. Wider school choice merely opens up some of these same opportunities to less affluent families, proponents contend. In addition, they say, school choice can better serve the disparate needs of heterogeneous students than can the stereotypical "one-size-fits-all" school administered by district officials. Finally, proponents argue that greater competition among public—and perhaps private—schools for students will boost the quality of education through competitive pressures.

Opponents of school choice enumerate several problems. An expanded system of choice could leave some students behind, possibly in failing schools. Choice, they argue, by allowing students to leave their local schools at will, could result in the resegregation of the nation's schools along lines of race, ethnicity, and socioeconomic status.

Although the term "choice" can also encompass voucher programs, which provide public subsidies for students to attend private schools, and which have been implemented in several cities nationwide, such programs are limited in scope. Rather, various forms of *public* school choice, such as traditional busing, magnet schools, open-enrollment programs, and, more recently, charter schools, provide the main form of school choice in America today and are likely to do so for some time to come. They are also the four options offered at the San Diego Unified School District (SDUSD), and so voucher programs are not a part of this study.

Focus of This Report

We focus on three related but broader issues of school choice:

- How students make decisions about whether to leave their local school.
- How school choice programs affect the level of integration among students, not just along lines of race and ethnicity but also along lines of academic achievement, language, and socioeconomic status.
- The effects on reading and math achievement for students who choose to leave their local schools.

Our findings on these issues should be of interest to audiences well beyond San Diego. In California as a whole, state mandates have led to a proliferation of charter schools and open-enrollment programs in other districts, and these are found in many other states across the county.

In addition, the mandates of federal No Child Left Behind (NCLB) legislation give every local, state, and federal education policymaker and administrator an urgent new reason to pay attention to the effect of school choice on achievement and integration. The federal rules require that schools that do not meet NCLB criteria offer busing to their students to allow them to transfer to better performing schools. And, for schools that fail to improve, another NCLB option is to close and reopen as a charter school.

School Choice in San Diego

SDUSD is the second-largest district in California and the eighth-largest district nationwide. Its students are quite diverse in terms of race, ethnicity, and socioeconomic status. For instance, no race or ethnicity comes close to being a majority of the student population (Hispanics form the largest group at roughly one-third of the student population in a typical year).

The district has implemented four main types of public school choice:

- The Voluntary Ethnic Enrollment Program (VEEP) is a voluntary busing program that has roots in a 1970s court order to desegregate the district, and it survives to this day.
- The district's magnet program also originates from court orders to desegregate schools. It gives students across the district a chance to attend a magnet school that has a specific academic focus or program, such as bilingual programs and performing arts.
- The Choice program is a state-mandated open-enrollment program (referred to in this report as "open-enrollment," "Choice," or sometimes both). Unlike VEEP and magnet programs, the Choice program does not provide busing to students.
- Finally, SDUSD hosts a growing number of charter schools. These schools are open to all students and are allowed to operate in a relatively autonomous way from the district administration.

Overall, SDUSD has a rather high percentage of students in choice programs. In 2003–2004, 28 percent of its students were attending nonlocal schools through the VEEP, magnet, or open-enrollment Choice programs or, alternatively, were enrolled in charter schools. Figure S.1 compares the share of district students in local schools and in each of these four choice programs in the 2001–2002 and 2003–2004 school years.[1]

The district conducts random drawings for admission to the VEEP, magnet, and the open-enrollment Choice programs; the lottery method allows us to compare outcomes for those randomly chosen to enroll and those not chosen. This provides us with an unusually clean way to evaluate the effect of winning one of these lotteries.

---

[1] The figure also shows another category, which is busing provided under the requirements of the federal No Child Left Behind law to students at schools that fail to make adequate yearly progress in achievement over two consecutive years. As shown in the figure, virtually no students enrolled in this option during the period we study and so we do not focus on this type of choice.

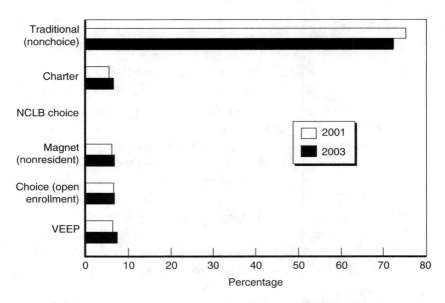

Figure S.1—Proportion of SDUSD Enrollment in Regular Schools and in Various School Choice Programs, 2001–2002 and 2003–2004 School Years

Similarly, charter schools are required by law to conduct lotteries in cases where demand exceeds the supply of slots. However, these lotteries are conducted not centrally but on a school-specific basis. Therefore, we assess the effect of charter schools by comparing the achievement growth of students during years they attend charters to their growth during years when they attend noncharter public schools. Both approaches improve considerably on early research methods that typically compared students in choice programs to students who remained at their local schools—either those at the "sending" schools or those who were already enrolled at the schools that received students through the busing program. Such a method creates a classic case of comparing apples to oranges—that is, the "apples"—students who choose to be bused—could differ in important but unobservable ways from the "oranges," the students in the comparison group, which could consist of those students who stay behind or new classmates at the receiving schools.

Who Exercises Choice in San Diego and Why

Our first research goal is to understand what causes an individual student to exercise choice by applying to leave his or her current school. Chapter 2 focuses on which students apply to the alternative programs that SDUSD offers and what they seem to be looking for in a new school. This task was made easier by the availability of centralized data on all applications in the centrally administered VEEP, magnet, and open-enrollment Choice programs in San Diego.

Our results provide some support for the argument that choice programs are skimming off high-ability students, but the evidence is fairly weak. In many instances, students with high test scores and high levels of parental education are found to be no more likely than their peers to apply to school choice programs. Patterns related to students' grade point averages are decidedly mixed. For all three of these variables—test scores, GPA, and parental education levels—even when the results are positive and statistically significant, the magnitude of the effects is relatively small.

One of the strongest results of our applicant analysis is that nonwhite students are generally more likely to participate than whites. Blacks in particular show strong propensities for applying to school choice programs and at the high school level, all nonwhite groups show a stronger probability than whites of applying. For example, the overall application rate to VEEP for our high school sample is 3.4 percent but in our models, after controlling for all other observable characteristics, we find that blacks have a probability of applying that is 3 percentage points higher than that for whites. These numbers suggest that black students are almost twice as likely as white students to apply to VEEP.

In the lower grades, however, the results on student race are somewhat weaker for Hispanics, and Asians show modest negative differences from whites. The good news for those concerned about the effect of choice on integration is that overall, nonwhite students clearly stand to gain from any benefits that school choice programs may provide.

Despite these indicators, one group that seems to be frequently left out is English learners (ELs), defined by the state as students who speak a language other than English at home and who are not fluent in English. However, the magnitude of the results is relatively modest, and at the middle school level, English learners are actually more likely to apply for one of the programs—VEEP—than non-EL students.

Using Choice to Improve the Academic Environment

Some proponents of school choice have argued that choice programs will increase academic achievement districtwide by increasing competition among schools. We cannot address this question directly with data from just one district. However, such competition is likely to arise if students are actually choosing schools based on academic criteria. Our findings suggest that academic factors, such as class sizes, test scores, student demographics, and teacher credentials, at the local school and at option schools, only moderately influence students' decisions to apply. The strongest evidence that students consider academic criteria when applying to alternative programs is that high school students are less likely to apply to any of the school choice programs if their local school has higher test scores.

There is some evidence that the distance between the student's neighborhood and a given option school has a deterrent effect on the probability of applying. In addition, that effect is found to be greatest for the one program that does not provide busing, the open-enrollment Choice program. However, these patterns are seen only at the elementary and high school levels.

Effect of Choice on Integration

In Chapter 3 we examine the effects of the three choice programs on integration in SDUSD. We go considerably beyond the traditional question of racial integration to examine also the integration of students by test scores, parental education levels, and language status.

We find that overall, choice programs integrate the district in terms of race/ethnicity and parental education but segregate the district in terms of test scores and EL versus non-EL students.

Student application behavior paints the clearest picture of the demand for school choice in SDUSD. We find that students who apply to choice programs appear to use these programs to improve the socioeconomic status of their peer group—changing that peer group by changing schools. In racial/ethnic terms, this means that applicants use choice programs to attend schools that are "more white." Of course, we cannot say that families are specifically concerned about race, given that race and ethnicity are correlated with many different characteristics in complex ways. Applicants also use these programs to attend schools that have a higher proportion of above-median test-score performers, more students who have highly educated parents, and fewer students who are English learners. Again, all of these variables are correlated, so care must be taken not to infer, for instance, that students and their families care specifically about the share of English learners in a school's student body.

Across all of the choice programs and all grade spans in SDUSD, the demand for choice exceeds the supply. Because the number of applications greatly exceeds the number of slots available, the actual number of school transfers, and the amount of integration that occurs, is far less than implied by the number of applications alone.

For example, if all the applications by black students to the VEEP program had been accepted, and all of these black students had then switched schools, these black students would experience a 48.2 percent increase in the number of white students in their school. However, VEEP's supply constraint reduces the change in percentage of white students to just 10.9 percent. Some of the schools that are mainly white are also the most heavily oversubscribed, so that few applicants win admission through the lottery. Furthermore, not all those students who are accepted actually transfer. This reduces the increase of white students in the black applicants' schools to 6.6 percent. Results are similar for other comparisons based on race/ethnicity.

We find that supply constraints cause similar reductions in integration by parental education. Evidence on integration by test scores is somewhat mixed. However, in our analysis of integration by English-learner status, we show that supply constraints ultimately serve to reduce the segregating effect of attempts by non-EL students to distance themselves from EL students.

Overall, the choice programs generally increase overall integration in terms of race/ethnicity and parental education. However, in most cases and along most dimensions, VEEP does the most to integrate and the open-enrollment Choice program does the least.

Effects of Choice on Reading and Math Achievement

For the VEEP, magnet, and open-enrollment Choice programs, which used a centralized lottery to admit students, we adopted a quasi-experimental approach in which we compared test scores in reading and math of applicants who won the lottery and applicants who lost the lottery. As detailed in Chapter 4, we examined students' achievement one, two, and three years after the lottery was held, in spring 2001 for fall 2001 admissions. We used two state tests, the California Standards Test (CST), a criterion-referenced test that evaluates a student's mastery of the state content standards, and a number of norm-referenced tests that compare students' performance to performance in a nationally normed sample of students. Using regression models, we tested whether the various math and reading test scores in spring 2002, 2003, and 2004 differed significantly between those who won the lottery and those who lost.

In the vast majority of cases, we found no evidence that winners and losers of a given lottery fared differently in these achievement tests one to three years after the admissions lottery was conducted. We interpret this to mean that winning a lottery neither helps nor hurts achievement growth.

There were two very important exceptions to this conclusion. First, in high schools, winners of lotteries for magnets performed significantly better on the CST math sections two and three years after the lottery took place. The gains were meaningful in size. There is a very good chance that this increased achievement can be causally attributed to magnet schools, because at the time of the lotteries in 2001, the only systematic difference between winners and losers of the magnet lotteries was the luck of the draw.

The second important exception is that in several cases, we detected statistically significant evidence that lottery winners underperformed in reading or math one year after winning the lottery but then made up this gap by the second year. This pattern, which is suggestive of a dislocation effect that temporarily affects student learning after the student switches schools, occurred only in a handful of cases.

Figure S.2 graphs estimated effects of winning a lottery on math CST scores one to three years after the lottery and illustrates the main conclusions we have just summarized. The figure shows three separate panels for VEEP, magnet, and open-enrollment Choice lotteries. The bars in each graph show the sample size available for the regression model; the sample size can be read off the left-hand axis of each graph. In most cases, our sample numbers in the hundreds or thousands of students. The clear exception is VEEP elementary school applications. In this specific case, we need to be clear that our limited sample size makes it less likely that we could detect any but the biggest of causal effects of winning a lottery.

The "crosses" in the figure show the estimated effect of winning a lottery and the confidence interval. The first thing that becomes apparent is that the estimated effects of winning a lottery are typically quite small, ranging from −0.1 to +0.1 of a standard deviation. Such effects, especially three years into an intervention, are considered quite modest.

The standard approach in statistics is to assume that the actual effect is zero and to reject this hypothesis only if the 95 percent confidence interval does not include zero. As shown in the figure, there are only a few cases where this confidence interval does not include zero. We have already described these cases in which there is a statistically significant effect.

First, the results suggest that winning a magnet lottery at the high school level is associated with positive gains in math achievement two and three years later. As shown in the middle panel, the size of the effects is meaningful, at roughly 0.2 of a standard deviation in test scores. Also, in middle schools, winning either the VEEP or Choice lotteries is associated with slightly lower math achievement in 2001–2002, one year after the lottery. However, in later years the effect becomes insignificantly different from zero.

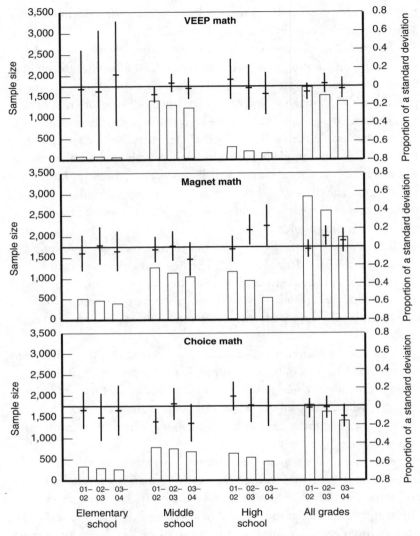

NOTES: In the graphs, the horizontal line on each "cross" shows the estimated effect of winning a school choice lottery, measured in standard deviations; the corresponding vertical line shows the 95 percent confidence interval. The bars show the sample sizes used in the underlying regression and the scale for this is found on the left-hand side of each graph.

Figure S.2—Models of the Effects of Winning School Choice Lotteries on CST Math Achievement: Effect Sizes, Confidence Intervals, and Regression Sample Sizes

Charter Schools and Achievement Levels

As we describe in Chapter 5, San Diego has an unusually rich concentration of charter schools. On average, these charter schools serve student populations that are more likely than their traditional public school counterparts to be economically disadvantaged, black, or Hispanic.

Unlike VEEP and open-enrollment programs (and to a certain extent magnet schools), charter schools enroll only or mostly students who have applied, not a mix of local students and choice applicants. It is therefore important to understand what distinguishes them from regular public schools. To this end, we conducted a survey of charter school administrators in San Diego. Many charter schools draw students from the entire San Diego metropolitan area, perhaps owing to their unique curricular emphases. Teachers at charter schools are younger, less educated, and less experienced than teachers at traditional schools, and this gap is particularly pronounced at the high school level. Class sizes in charter schools are roughly the same as in traditional schools. Because teacher salaries are the primary cost of running a school, one could infer that charter schools spend less than regular public schools on the daily running of a school. Conversely, some charters have to spend significantly more than the typical public school to pay for physical space.

Although the district does not conduct a centralized random drawing for charter schools, we are able to estimate the effect of attending a charter by looking for changes in trends in a student's test scores during years when the student switches into or out of a charter school. This approach eliminates the need to compare students who do and do not choose charters; these two groups might differ in important but unobservable ways.

We do not find strong evidence that charter school students are uniformly over- or underperforming. Performance appears to differ by both grade span and subject. Performance also appears to depend on whether the charter school has converted from regular public school status or represents an entirely new startup charter school. Elementary startup charter schools typically underperform in their first few years of operation but appear to catch up to traditional schools after the third year. Conversion schools—regular public schools that convert into charters, often retaining teachers and serving the same student population at the same school site, but no longer bound by district regulations governing standard schools—appear to underperform regular public schools in elementary school math and middle school reading but overperform in middle school math. Classroom characteristics, such as teacher qualifications and class size, do not explain much of the similarities or differences in achievement across the two areas.

These findings suggest that policymakers could benefit from a detailed comparative analysis of the revenue streams and costs of charter schools and traditional public schools. Charter schools appear to have less money available to spend in the classroom and so they must hire teachers with significantly less experience and education than the teachers that noncharter public schools can hire. Because it appears that the charter schools are performing at comparable levels, it is possible that charter schools in San Diego are somewhat more cost-effective than traditional public schools.

Our findings that in some cases conversion charters and startup charters perform differently raise questions about other aspects of charters that matter for student performance. Over time, as new charters are created and existing charters fine-tune their academic approaches, we may be better able to explain variations in charter school outcomes. Additionally, it is of crucial importance to learn more about the types of students who benefit the most from attending charter schools. There is some evidence in our data that the effects of attending a charter school differ by race and ethnicity. More research is required to learn more about why these differences exist.

Conclusion and Policy Implications

Broadly speaking, this report examines two questions. First: Has school choice in San Diego served to integrate the city's schools, both racially and socioeconomically, or has it served only to skim off affluent white students or high-scoring students into elite schools of choice, thereby increasing social stratification throughout the district? The second question is: How have the various choice programs affected the math and reading achievement of participants?

Our results seem particularly clearcut on the first question of integration. We found a positive relationship, although weak, between the probability of applying to a choice program and a student's test scores and parental education levels; the evidence of the relationship between a student's GPA and probability of application was mixed. In addition, our analysis of both applications and actual school transfers makes it quite clear that the choice programs in San Diego do serve to integrate the city's schools racially and socioeconomically. Our analysis of the student demography at charter schools makes clear that charters in San Diego do not fit the stereotype of elite schools skimming off primarily white, affluent, and high-scoring students.

In spite of this general conclusion—that choice programs in SDUSD have integrated students along many dimensions—there are two important qualifications here.

First, the program that clearly has done the least to integrate students is the open-enrollment Choice program. Perhaps it is not a coincidence that this program does not provide busing. One possible interpretation is that the provision of busing is an important mechanism to level the playing field in school choice. In less affluent families, parents (or a single parent) may lack access to private transportation or may lack the time to drive their children to distant schools and so could find it infeasible to send their children to a school choice program. However, a second factor may also be at play. The open-enrollment Choice program allows unfettered access by any student to any (nonmagnet) school, whereas both VEEP and magnet programs have built-in mechanisms aimed at promoting integration. It could well be that such mechanisms are needed to ensure that school choice programs lead to meaningful amounts of integration.

A second interpretation stems from our documentation that even in a district like San Diego, which has quite high participation in choice programs, space limitations sharply reduce the degree to which integration actually occurs. Application patterns show that nonwhite students, students whose parents have less education, and students with lower test scores want to move to nonlocal schools to a degree that far surpasses what the existing choice programs can fulfill. This is a fairly remarkable finding, given that by 2003–2004, 28 percent of district students were already in various choice programs.

As for the second and larger question of student achievement, the best conclusion seems to be that *in most cases,* students who win lotteries to attend a school through VEEP, magnet, or Choice programs, or who switch into charters, show no statistically significant difference in reading and math achievement.

There are numerous exceptions, but two patterns stand out in a statistical sense. First, magnet high schools seem to produce higher math achievement. Second, in some grades and subjects in all the programs, students switching into the programs sometimes suffer temporary, typically one-year, declines in achievement. This is quite consonant with the recent literature on charter schools in other states.

Implications of Choice Popularity in San Diego

We are left with an important policy question. More than one-quarter of the district's students participate in choice programs, and a large number of applicants are turned away for lack of space. Why are the four school choice programs so popular when they seem to produce no additional growth in math and reading achievement over that in students' local schools?

Several answers come to mind, each with quite different implications. The first and clearly most disturbing theory is that parents overestimate the academic benefits from the choice program and so base their school choice decisions on erroneous beliefs. The district's Enrollment Options Office annually mails a detailed school choice brochure to each family in the district describing the academic curriculum of each magnet school. But even this information cannot directly signal the elusive concept of "school quality." Similarly, test scores are widely available, but even a sophisticated layperson could confuse a high level of test scores at a school with school quality. In reality, outside factors, such as parental background, might be responsible in part for high test scores. A second explanation might be that improved math and reading achievement may not be the most important parental goal and that many other aspects of a school's environment matter to parents as well. Schools are not, after all, test-score factories that do nothing but boost academic achievement. Our evidence and that of other studies indicate that parents care deeply about the socioeconomic status of their children's schoolmates. Parents may view this as an end in itself or as a means to a better future for their children.

Larger Implications and Questions

What are the policy implications for policymakers, both locally and nationally? The first is that school choice programs can indeed promote integration. Two policy levers appear to have increased the level of integration created by choice. The first is busing, so that students from less affluent families can get to their chosen school. Another is a system of pairing schools or the setting of quotas at each receiving school for students from various geographic areas.

What are the larger implications of the nondefinitive test-score results? It would be extremely premature to argue that they suggest that the school choice programs should be either curtailed or expanded. To some readers, the very fact that the programs are so popular with parents may be sufficient justification to continue them. To others, the lack of a consistently positive effect of choice on reading and math achievement may be quite troubling. But potentially mitigating factors abound here. Do the reading and math tests capture true achievement well? What about achievement in other domains? What about nonacademic outcomes? Charter schools may actually receive less funding than regular public schools and so they may prove more cost-effective even though they seem to produce about the same achievement gains as regular public schools. For open-enrollment Choice, which does not provide subsidized busing, the costs of transportation are borne by the family, so if the family wants to enroll a child, what is the public cost, if any? For the two programs with subsidized busing (VEEP and magnets), cost does become more of a concern. The positive results in math for magnet high schools insulate magnets somewhat. For VEEP, the issue of cost-effectiveness is perhaps most relevant.

Our findings are likely to prove useful to other districts as they think about their own choice programs, but there is a larger national implication as well. The NCLB legislation requires that districts devote some of their Title I funds to provide busing for students in schools that have failed to meet "adequate yearly progress" standards two years in a row. This requirement would allow those students to attend "nonfailing" schools. SDUSD has implemented this requirement by combining NCLB busing with its preexisting VEEP busing routes.

It seems likely that the outcomes for these NCLB-busing participants will resemble what we have found for VEEP participants in San Diego. The key national policy question then becomes this: If NCLB is concerned about boosting academic achievement in math, reading, and related core subjects, will busing provide the most cost-effective way to help students in low-performing schools? This debate could well become one of the central education policy issues nationwide by the time NCLB is up for reauthorization in 2007.

Contents

Web-Only Appendix
> *This web-only appendix is available at http://www.ppic.org/content/
> other/806JBR_web_only_appendix.pdf*

Figures

Tables

Web-Only Appendix Tables

Acknowledgments

Given the many facets of school choice within the San Diego Unified School District, we relied on a number of individuals for their insight, experience, and advice. We would like to thank former Superintendent Alan Bersin, now California's Secretary of Education, for granting us access to the data and staff. Karen Bachofer, Executive Director of Standards, Assessment, and Accountability, provided much useful assistance and feedback on our research throughout the entire project. We would also like to thank Sandra Robles and Patricia Trandal, current and former staff members, respectively, at the Enrollment Options Office for taking considerable time to explain how the lottery system works and allowing us to work with the data. Without their support, this project would have been much more difficult. We thank Brian Bennett, formerly at the Office of School Choice, for his insights on charter schools. We also thank Peter Bell and Jeff Jones from the Research and Reporting Department for their assistance with the student data and test scores, Susie Millett for helpful discussions on school choice, and Charles Rynerson, formerly from the Instructional Facilities Planning Department, for information and expertise on school feeder patterns. Thanks also to Brad Lewis for assistance with calculating distances between schools.

A number of people provided invaluable advice relating to the design of our survey of charter schools. Brian Bennett, formerly of SDUSD, as well as Julie Umansky and Collin Miller of the California Charter Schools Association reviewed an early draft of the survey, and the final version of the survey was reviewed and approved by Brian Bennett's advisory group of principals/directors. We are grateful to the many charter school administrators and leaders who took the time to fill out the survey.

This report has received generous funding from the Smith Richardson Foundation, Inc., the Girard Foundation, and the Public

Policy Institute of California (PPIC). Mark Steinmeyer and Phoebe Cottingham (current and former senior program officers at the Smith Richardson Foundation); Susan Wolking, Executive Director of the Girard Foundation; and Max Neiman and Paul G. Lewis (current and former program directors for the Governance and Education Programs at PPIC) have provided many helpful ideas.

We thank Richard Greene and Patricia Bedrosian for expert editorial assistance. Administrative support was provided by numerous staff members at PPIC.

The database used in this project builds on a large database that a PPIC team led by Julian Betts has been working on since 2000. We warmly acknowledge funders of our previous projects whose funding created the infrastructure that made the current project feasible: PPIC, The William and Flora Hewlett Foundation, and The Atlantic Philanthropies. In addition, at the University of California, San Diego, Dean Paul Drake of the Division of Social Sciences kindly provided space for the overall SDUSD project since its inception in 2000. Without all of this support, this report would not have been possible.

We are indebted to our reviewers: Jaime Calleja Alderete, Ken Hall, Paul Hill, Christopher Jepsen, and Mark Schneider. Valuable comments on an earlier version of Chapter 2 were also provided by Steven Erie, Christopher Jepsen, Steven Raphael, James Rauch, Jon Sonstelie, and Christopher Woodruff.

Any opinions or interpretations expressed in this report are those of the authors alone and do not necessarily reflect the views of the Public Policy Institute of California.

1. School Choice in San Diego and Nationwide: An Introduction and Overview

School choice is a policy issue with a long history. Court-ordered busing designed to reduce racial segregation became common throughout the nation in the 1970s as a way to equalize school quality between whites and blacks. Lukas (1985) gives a riveting account of the political tensions that busing created in Boston, culminating in riots in 1974. Nationwide, dozens of court-ordered mandatory busing programs similar to the one in Boston have gradually evolved into nonmandatory systems of interschool choice and related magnet school programs. These descendants of court-ordered busing have continued to this day as voluntary ways to give parents some choice among public schools for their children. Recently, charter schools, and in a few locations vouchers, have provided additional types of school choice.

All these forms of school choice have attracted controversy. There should be little wonder why school choice continues to attract so much attention. In the United States, schools vary radically in quality, and without some form of choice, public school students are limited to schools in their own neighborhoods. A lack of choice hurts students who live in areas with low-performing schools. More often than not, the affected students are economically disadvantaged, Hispanic, black, or Indochinese, and, especially in California, English learners.

The controversy over school choice has gained new momentum with the passage in 2001 of the federal No Child Left Behind (NCLB) law. NCLB focuses interventions on schools receiving federal Title I funding that fail for two consecutive years to make adequate yearly progress, meaning that an insufficient number of students or subgroups of students have met state-defined standards in reading or math proficiency.

1

These schools must allow low-performing students to choose to attend another school in the district, with the district providing busing. NCLB also mandates another option for failing schools—to convert into a charter school, thus representing a second school choice mechanism embedded in the federal law.

Probably the most controversial and perhaps best known type of school choice is a voucher system, which allows parents to use public money to send their children to private schools often affiliated with established religions. In spite of the 2002 U.S. Supreme Court *Zelman v. Simmons-Harris* decision allowing public money to be spent on vouchers for private school tuition, it seems clear that the voucher form of school choice will not prevail in the next few years: Many states have constitutional prohibitions on such plans that are stronger than the provisions in the U.S. Constitution. It could take years to resolve these issues at the state level. Moreover, voters do not seem ready to support private school vouchers. In 2000, for instance, voters in California decisively rejected Proposition 38, a private school voucher ballot initiative. The measure received only 29 percent support.

Current School Choice Options

Several other forms of school choice, although not the subject of virulent debates in the op-ed pages, have already quietly been providing large numbers of students with alternatives to their local neighborhood schools. Many states, including California, have implemented an open-enrollment policy that allows students to apply to any school they choose within a school district. Busing exists in many urban districts, typically originating in court desegregation orders. Additionally, many districts have created magnet schools to attract diverse groups of students to a given campus. Finally, charter schools represent a relatively new but quickly growing type of public school choice.

We know surprisingly little about these widespread forms of school choice. Among the unanswered questions are: Who chooses open enrollment, magnets, charters, and more traditional busing programs? How does choice change the extent of student integration in terms of race/ethnicity, socioeconomic status, and language? Do students who transfer under these programs gain academically? If so, why? Which types of students gain the most from these choice programs? Are the programs truly reducing the achievement gap between affluent and less affluent students? How could administrators improve the programs' effectiveness? Research on these issues has been lacking.

To understand why these questions are so important, it is useful to survey the national controversy surrounding school choice.

The Current Policy Debate over School Choice

Advocates of the various forms of school choice view them as a way to improve schools in general and to reduce the disparities between students in affluent and less affluent areas. Underlying this is a concern for relatively disadvantaged students who, it is argued, often attend local schools that are of poor quality. If students' destinies are largely determined by the quality of their local schools, then why not give motivated students whose local schools are failing a chance to attend a better school elsewhere? Disadvantaged students stand to gain considerably from this expanded choice, proponents argue. A second argument is that decentralized school control will ensue from a system of choice, which in turn should generate a greater variety of curricula and pedagogical methods to cater to the heterogeneous needs of students. A key advantage of decentralization is that it improves the flow of information between families and school providers; it is difficult for a central district administration to react quickly to the needs of students and families without a massive investment in surveys or parent interviews. A third argument is that active competition among schools for students might improve the quality of *all* schools by creating a market environment that forces substandard schools to improve or lose students.

Most objections to school choice generally have centered on its more radical forms, such as the use of publicly funded vouchers that would allow students to attend private schools; some extreme school choice schemes envision the complete privatization of schools. Critics worry that these forms of choice would simply replicate the existing inequalities, with well-to-do families sending their students to the most exclusive private schools by topping up their public voucher money out of their own pockets. Other concerns are that the public school system represents the only existing example of the cultural "melting pot," and that a system of complete private choice would lead to greater segregation than currently exists along a variety of lines—economic, racial/ethnic, cultural, and religious. Another criticism of a partially privatized system is that publicly funded vouchers could drain resources away from public schools, hurting educational quality for those left behind.

A quite separate line of criticism of school choice maintains that the real solution to the problem of low and unequal academic achievement in our schools is simply to spend more. Choice, in this view, is a red herring. But empirical evidence is not compelling; it does not show that dollars alone can do much to improve student achievement on average or that money alone can narrow the achievement gap between affluent and less affluent students.[1] Betts and Danenberg (2001) present calculations suggesting that even large injections of money would not equalize achievement across California's schools. The main obstacle is the large gaps in achievement related to students' socioeconomic status (Betts, Rueben, and Danenberg, 2000; Coley, 2002). In the end, even large infusions of cash into the public school system are unlikely by themselves to eliminate these achievement gaps across all schools. The clear implication is that other reforms, including school choice, must remain on the table as long as there is a case to be made that they could boost average achievement or reduce disparities in achievement.

Research on School Choice Effects

Although public school choice exists and is much more prevalent than commonly realized, we know very little about its effects.

Roughly speaking, there have been two waves of research on the effects of school choice. One arose from traditional busing programs intended to reduce racial segregation that have existed for three decades

---

[1]For reviews of the effect of school resources, such as spending per pupil on student achievement and on students' ultimate years of schooling and earnings after leaving school, see Hanushek (1996) and Betts (1996), respectively. In the California context, see Betts, Rueben, and Danenberg (2000), Jepsen and Rivkin (2002), and Betts, Zau, and Rice (2003). Betts, Zau, and King (2005) study a massive literacy intervention in San Diego and find that in many cases it did narrow gaps in achievement among students, but even the large expenditures accompanying this program could not come close to eliminating disparities in achievement among students.

or more in many states. Many studies, most done in the 1970s and early 1980s, examined the effectiveness of these programs. But we argue that almost none of these studies has anything convincing to say about whether busing improves outcomes for bused students or has effects on the populations in the sending and receiving schools.

Several good reviews of this literature (e.g., Crain and Mahard, 1981; Cook et al., 1984) show that the vast majority of studies are observational, lacking a valid comparison or "control" group. For instance, many of the earlier studies compare students who were bused with those who remained behind. But if those who volunteered for busing differed in unobservable ways from those who did not volunteer, we cannot reliably disentangle the effects of busing from the effects of these unobserved differences.

A convincing and fully legitimate measure of the causal effect of busing requires a valid comparison group, preferably accomplished through some sort of randomization. For example, if there were a lottery for busing, with some students who apply being randomly chosen for the busing program, then those students who "lost" the lottery would provide a valid comparison group. On average, they would have the same observed and unobserved characteristics (including motivation and learning aptitude) as the students from the same applicant pool who are randomly chosen to be bused. This randomization removes the "apples and oranges" problem inherent in the bulk of the busing literature.

Crain and Mahard (1981) find only two cases nationally in which busing was performed using randomization (Mahan and Mahan, 1970; and Zdep, 1971). Although their results showed some minor gains in achievement, it seems obvious that a handful of experiments involving a few hundred students in the 1960s does not provide a good guide for policy decisions that need to be made about today's quite distinct choice programs in California or elsewhere in the United States. Moreover, the racial/ethnic and language mix that exists in the state and country today stands in stark contrast to that of the 1960s. The goals of school choice and busing have also changed markedly.

A second and more recent literature on school choice has tended to use more convincing methodologies, although the same lack of randomization has made it difficult to learn as much as we would like.

For example, early research reports on the Milwaukee private school voucher program drew radically varying conclusions. Over time, it has become clear to outside researchers that the source of the disagreement stems from variations in the comparison group chosen by each set of researchers.

Some of the most recent work on vouchers has used randomization (see for instance Howell and Peterson, 2002; Mayer et al., 2002). This work has been challenged on a number of technical grounds, such as a lack of robustness to alternative definitions of race and choice of samples (Krueger and Zhu, 2003).

One notable recent paper examines public school choice using quasi-experimental methods. Cullen, Jacob, and Levitt (2003) study an open-enrollment program at the high school level in Chicago public schools. They take advantage of the lotteries used to draw from the applicant pool, in this way solving the apples and oranges problem. They find little evidence that this program improved student achievement.

Charter School Research

Similarly, early work on charter schools, although extremely useful, has not fully dealt with the selective nature by which students apply to charter schools (and in many instances the selective nature by which charter schools admit students). The best of this work has avoided comparing students at charters and regular public schools and has instead followed individual students as they switch between regular public schools and charters, or vice versa. This method tests whether the test-score trajectory of individual students alters after these switches. But this literature is still quite small.

Gill et al. (2001) give a sobering account of the limits of our knowledge about vouchers for either private schools or charter schools.

Contributions of the Present Report

The present report uses data from the San Diego Unified School District (SDUSD) to study three related issues: the decision to leave the local school, the effects on integration, and the effects on achievement for those who switch schools.

The report fills several gaps in knowledge about school choice. It documents exactly who opts for school choice and the types of schools that are chosen. Second, it makes use of an unusual *random drawing procedure* that SDUSD uses to determine which applicants are accepted to its open enrollment, busing, and magnet programs. This randomization solves the apples and oranges problem inherent in most of the earlier literature by providing a valid comparison group against which to compare those who are randomly chosen to participate in the programs. Further, because we use a rich longitudinal dataset, we are able in theory to open up the black box of school choice to determine which aspects of switching schools, such as changes in curriculum, teacher qualifications, class size, or peer groups, contribute most strongly to increasing the academic achievement of school choice participants. Third, on the question of integration, we extend the analysis beyond the traditional focus on race and ethnicity by also studying integration based on language, socioeconomic status, and test scores. We also examine how the limited supply of spaces in the various choice programs reduces the amount of integration that occurs relative to the demand expressed in applications by students, many of whom do not win in the lotteries. This is an important issue to study because proponents and opponents often debate what more widespread forms of school choice, such as universally provided busing, might do to attempt to integrate public schools.

We also study the effect of charter schools on achievement. However, because the district does not conduct a centralized lottery for admission to charter schools, we cannot use the quasi-experimental approach described above. We use what many consider a next-best method—a fixed-effect approach that makes each student his or her own comparison group. This is accomplished by comparing test-score growth in years the student is in a charter school to years that he or she is in a regular public school.

One advantage of the present study is that SDUSD is a very large and diverse district with a large number of students entering choice programs each year. Our available sample size is quite large compared to the more highly publicized voucher programs. For example, the Milwaukee voucher program grew from a cap of 1,500 students before

1995 to 9,500 students in 2000–2001, whereas the Cleveland Scholarship and Tutoring Grant Program enrolled only 3,764 students in 1998–1999. Florida's school voucher program attracted only 57 students in its first two years and has recently been overturned in state court (see Gill et al., 2001, Chapter Two).

The combined enrollment in these programs, at roughly 13,000, is dwarfed by the existing public school choice programs in SDUSD, where more than 35,000 students participated in school choice programs in 2001–2002 alone. Not only are SDUSD's programs larger, but they are unlikely to face continued challenges on the grounds that they violate state or federal constitutions, since they do not involve the use of public money for private institutions.

San Diego's Choice Programs in Detail

The choice programs in San Diego are larger than most people realize, with fully one-quarter of students in SDUSD enrolled in one of these choice programs during the school years that we study, 2001–2002 through 2003–2004.

Open Enrollment

California has an open-enrollment policy that allows students to apply to any school within or outside their district, which the state calls the School Choice program. Subject to space availability, students can switch from their local schools to any other in the district (except magnet schools). Out-of-district applications are also accepted but are typically given lower priority. One notable limitation of this state program, at least in San Diego, is that many schools have few if any additional slots available. Another restriction is the time required to commute from the family home to a given school, which may prevent many students from applying, especially if the family is disadvantaged and lacks readily available private or public transportation.[2]

---

[2]For evidence that both car ownership and the quality of public transportation affect the probability of employment, see Raphael and Rice (2002) and Rice (2004). A similar link may exist between the availability of transportation and the exercise of families' school choice options.

VEEP

A second plan that exists alongside School Choice is the Voluntary Ethnic Enrollment Program (VEEP), SDUSD's busing program that originated from a mid-1970s court racial desegregation order. In VEEP, schools are grouped together into sets of allied patterns—small groups of schools with a mix of high and low percentages of whites. Originally, sending and receiving schools within VEEP were grouped so that the movement of a nonwhite student from any sending to any receiving school in the pattern would make the racial composition of the student body at both schools become more representative of the district's overall racial makeup. At present, however, VEEP has transformed so that a student of any race can apply to attend any school in the pattern. Nevertheless, schools are still matched into allied patterns based on racial composition, so that typically, but not always, this type of school choice should act to integrate schools racially. The district requires eight student applications before any new busing pattern is added between any two schools in the allied pattern. Another feature of allied patterns is that students in theory could choose to move from traditionally receiving schools to traditionally sending schools, although this is typically not seen. In practice, schools within an allied pattern that receive VEEP students from other schools are in more affluent areas with relatively high percentages of white students, and conversely for schools that are sending schools. Roughly half of the students in the district live in areas that have an active VEEP busing program.

Magnet Schools

A third component of choice in SDUSD is a host of magnet schools. Again, the historical origin of the magnet program was to provide innovative programs that would induce students to move among schools, making the racial composition of both the magnet (receiving) school and the sending school more representative of that of the district as a whole. Any student can apply to any magnet school.

Charter Schools

A fourth type of school choice consists of charter schools—deregulated schools that have been freed from many parts of the state education code. These schools are quite diverse in their goals.

Other Programs

A fifth type of school choice that began in 2002–2003 was busing provided to so-called failing schools under the federal NCLB law. In practice, this nascent form of school choice has been implemented by using, or if necessary modifying, the preexisting bus routes of VEEP. Because by 2003–2004 only 265 students had availed themselves of this opportunity, we do not discuss NCLB choice further in this report.

Similarities and Contrasts

The origin of each of these programs may have some bearing on their wider applicability. Choice, the statewide open-enrollment program, and charter schools both owe their existence to laws passed in Sacramento. Thus, their effectiveness should be of key interest to policymakers in Sacramento as well as to local policymakers and administrators throughout the state and in the many other states that have similar laws. The VEEP and magnet programs, on the other hand, grew out of court mandates and so may be of greater interest to districts around the country that share the history of having created similar choice programs under court order. In addition, existing busing programs like these are likely to become models for the newest form of school choice nationwide required by NCLB legislation. Another useful distinction among the programs is whether the students at a choice school attend because of the choice program or whether some or many students attend simply because it is their local school. Typically, applicants to the choice programs apply to move to a nonlocal school at which a majority of students are local residents. VEEP and Choice fit this description exactly. Most of the magnets fit this description as well, although a few magnets attract almost all of their students from other schools' attendance areas. Charter schools differ from these other programs in that all of the students explicitly apply to attend; there are no "local" students. In this sense, charter schools are unique in that they are *school-*

level forms of choice. But even here there are distinctions. Startup charters typically draw students from a wide area, whereas schools that have converted to charter status more typically draw many of their students from the local attendance area. This distinction is quite important because under the federal NCLB law, conversion to a charter school is one of the possible reforms for a school that has missed its achievement targets for six years in a row.

Admission to San Diego's School Choice Programs

For the VEEP, magnet, or open-enrollment programs, if a school receives more applications than it has spaces in a given grade, administrators hold a lottery. Each application is assigned a random number, and applications are ranked in this way. In addition, students are placed into priority groups based on factors such as whether a sibling already attends the school, the time of year at which the application was made, and whether the student is from the district or (extremely rarely) from outside the district.[3] The district does not conduct a centralized lottery for applications to charter schools, although charter schools are required by law to conduct a random drawing if demand exceeds the supply of slots.[4]

Each of the four larger types of school choice attracts roughly 5 to 6 percent of the district's students, so that overall about one in four SDUSD students participates in school choice. Figure 1.1 provides greater detail. As the figure shows, the share of students in nonlocal or charter schools has grown moderately during the three school years that we study, whereas the share in regular local schools has declined from 75 percent in 2001–2002 to 72 percent in 2003–2004. Clearly, school choice as a whole is very popular with families in San Diego.[5]

---

[3]Chapter 4 and Appendix C provide further details.

[4]Throughout this report, we refer to the selection procedure as being a series of lotteries, and to lottery winners and losers. Our use of these terms is intended to help the reader understand the procedure used for selecting students.

[5]For a more detailed account of the history of the various school choice programs, and the likely effects of the new NCLB choice program, see Zau and Betts (2005).

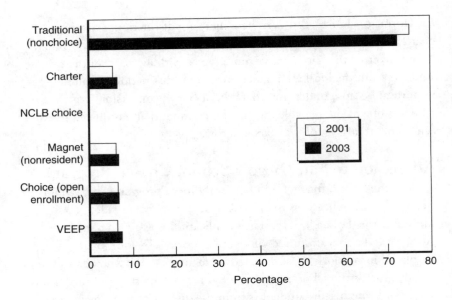

Figure 1.1—Proportion of SDUSD Enrollment in Regular Schools
and in Various School Choice Programs, 2001–2002 and
2003–2004 School Years

For the remainder of this report we will typically refer to the open-enrollment program known in California as School Choice simply as the "open-enrollment" or "open-enrollment Choice" program. However, for convenience we will refer to any nonlocal school available to a student through one of the four school choice options included in the analysis—open enrollment, VEEP, magnet, or charter—as a "choice school" or an "option school."

Outline of the Report

Chapter 2 examines which students exercise their option to leave their local school and why, using statistical models of the probability that students will apply to leave their local school. We study the relative importance of the student's characteristics, the characteristics of his or her local school, and the characteristics of the option schools to which he or she could apply.

Chapter 3 examines the effect of the VEEP, magnet, and open-enrollment programs on integration. It uses numerous ways to define groups, along lines of race/ethnicity, student achievement, parental education, and language status. A key innovation of this chapter is to compare the demand for school-switching, as expressed through the application process, with actual transfers. We study the extent to which the lotteries in oversubscribed schools and oversubscribed grades limit the expressed demand among students to move and the implications for integration.

Chapter 4 examines the effect of the VEEP, magnet, and open-enrollment programs on student achievement in math and reading. To do this, we compare the test scores of students who won and lost specific lotteries in spring 2001, following these students through the following three school years.

Chapter 5 studies San Diego's charter schools and, specifically, any gains in performance on math and reading tests from switching between regular public schools and charter schools. We begin by comparing charters to regular public schools and also report on a survey we conducted of charter school operators. We also devote considerable attention to the dynamics of charter schools—that is, whether new charters undergo teething pains, and whether students who switch into charters, or those who switch out, suffer temporary losses in their achievement growth related to their move between schools.

Chapter 6 concludes and draws lessons for policy.

2. Who Chooses to Apply to Public School Choice Programs and Why?

In this chapter, we use the district's data on applications to choice programs to identify which students apply and what characteristics they appear to be looking for in a school. Most previous research on this issue has used actual attendance data rather than application data (see, for example, Cullen, Jacob, and Levitt, 2003; Cullen, Jacob, and Levitt, 2000).[1] However, attendance data may not fully capture demand. If a school does not have enough space for all who apply, then attendance data will understate the actual demand. In fact, if highly sought-after schools have very few openings, then actual attendance data could lead to the conclusion that such schools are not highly in demand. Using application data allows us to net out the supply side of the issue and focus on the demand for school choice.

Our analysis includes three of the four choice programs: VEEP, magnets, and open enrollment. Applications to charter schools are not integrated into the district's centralized database, so charter schools are excluded from this analysis and are discussed separately in Chapter 5. The data used in this chapter are for school choice applications made during the 2000–2001 school year for entrance into choice schools in fall 2001. The data on the characteristics of the students and schools are from the 2000–2001 school year, when the students were making

---

[1]Reback (2005) uses application data rather than attendance data. However, he looks at the number of requests for transfers between districts rather than between schools, and his data are aggregated at the district level rather than at the individual student level. There is also a separate but relevant literature in the tradition of Tiebout (1956), which estimates demand for school quality by looking at changes in housing prices associated with the characteristics of the local school (see, for example, Black, 1999; Figlio and Lucas, 2004; Hoxby, 2000; Rothstein, 2004).

applications for the upcoming year. Further details about the data and methods used in the analysis can be found in Appendix A.

The multivariate probit models used in this chapter's analysis estimate how the probability of applying to a school choice program responds to various characteristics of the students and of the schools. The advantage of performing a multivariate analysis is that it allows us to estimate the effect of each individual component if we could hold all of the other components constant. In this way, we can see the individual effect of a particular student or school characteristic as distinct from any other characteristics that may be correlated with it.

The models used in the analysis measure how the probability of applying to one of the three choice programs is affected by the characteristics of the students, the characteristics of their local area schools, and the characteristics of the set of schools to which they can apply. The full results of the probit models are presented in Appendix Tables A.1 through A.3. Figures 2.1 through 2.3 show results for selected variables that had statistically significant results.

To put the magnitude of the predicted effects of changes in the explanatory variables into perspective, Table 2.1 presents the mean application rates among all eligible students, for each program in each grade span.

Table 2.1

Average Annual Application Rates
(percentage of eligible students applying)

	VEEP	Magnet	Choice
Elementary school	2.09	1.59	2.78
Middle school	6.74	4.04	3.12
High school	3.42	3.33	3.48

Which Students Apply to School Choice Programs?

Figure 2.1 illustrates the relative magnitudes of the effects of the student characteristics in each grade span and each program. We omit bars from the graph when the result is not statistically significant, i.e.,

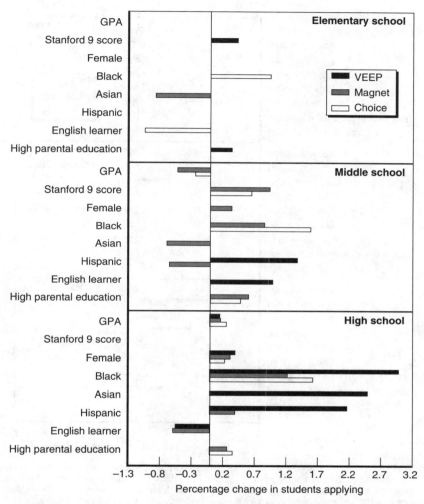

NOTES: The numbers on the horizontal axis are percentage changes in probability of application. The bars for the grade point average (GPA) and the Stanford 9 score depict the expected change in the probability of applying associated with a 0.5 increase in GPA and a 1 standard deviation increase in the Stanford 9 test score, respectively. The bars for the other variables show the expected difference in the probability of applying between the categories shown here and the relevant comparison group (male, white, non-English learner, or low parental education). All effects shown are statistically significant at the 10 percent level. The Choice program in this figure refers to the open-enrollment program.

Figure 2.1—Change in the Probability of Application Associated with Selected Student Characteristics

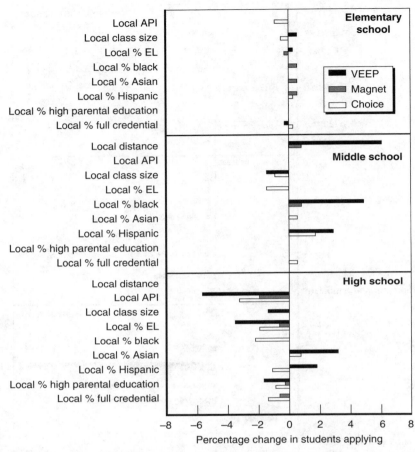

NOTES: The numbers on the horizontal axis are percentage changes in the probability of application. The bars for distance, Academic Performance Index (API), and class size depict the expected change associated with the local school being one mile farther away, a 100 point increase in API, or a two-student increase in class size, respectively. The bars for the student body demographic variables depict the expected change associated with a 10 percentage point increase in each variable. The final bar shows the expected change for a 3 percentage point increase in the percentage of teachers who hold full credentials. "Local distance" is not included for elementary students, because we use the local elementary school to proxy for all students' residences. All effects shown are statistically significant at the 10 percent level. The Choice program in this figure refers to the open-enrollment program.

Figure 2.2—Change in the Probability of Application Associated with
Local School Characteristics

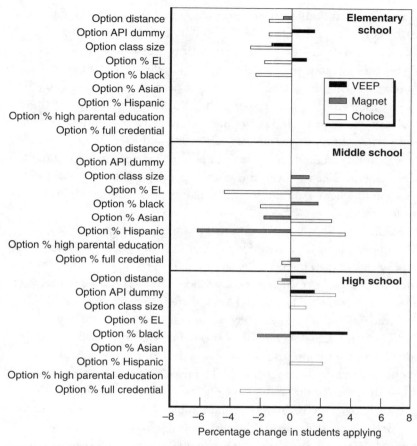

NOTES: The numbers on the horizontal axis are percentage changes in the probability of application. The bars for distance and class size depict the expected change from an increase of three miles or two students, respectively, for the weighted average across option schools in the program, where the weight is 1/distance-squared. The API dummy indicates that the weighted average API across option schools is higher than the API of the local school. (The API dummy is calculated slightly differently for the VEEP elementary school sample. See Appendix A for details.) The bars for the student body demographic variables depict the expected change associated with a 10 percentage point increase in the weighted average across the option schools in the program, and the final bar shows the expected change for a 3 percentage point increase in the percentage of teachers who hold full credentials. All effects shown are statistically significant at the 10 percent level. The Choice program in this figure refers to the open- enrollment program.

Figure 2.3—Change in the Probability of Application Associated with
Option School Characteristics

when the probit model fails to reject the hypothesis that the variable had no effect on the probability of applying. Several patterns emerge.

A potential criticism of choice programs is that they might draw high-achieving students away from schools in disadvantaged areas, thereby lowering the overall quality of the peer group in those schools and creating an even more impoverished learning atmosphere for those students who remain. In light of previous research that emphasizes the importance of peer group effects (Betts, Zau, and Rice, 2003), skimming of high-ability students could have important repercussions for student achievement. The results in this chapter provide mixed evidence on the question of whether choice programs mainly attract higher-ability students.

Figure 2.1 illustrates the expected change in probability of applying to a program from an increase in GPA of 0.5. For the high school grade span, students with higher GPAs are more likely to apply, although the effects are small.[2] At the elementary school level, GPA does not seem to matter, and at the middle school level, there is some evidence indicating that students are in fact less likely to apply if their GPAs are high.

The figure also illustrates the expected change in probability of applying to a program from a 1 standard deviation increase in the Stanford 9 standardized test score. The test-score variable that we use shows the mean of the student's math and reading scores from that test. In contrast to the GPA results, high Stanford 9 scores do not matter for the high school grade span. However, there is some evidence that test scores do matter at the elementary school level for the probability of applying to VEEP, and they also appear to matter at the middle school level for the probability of applying to a magnet or open-enrollment school. In any case, whenever the student's test-score measure has a statistically significant effect, that effect is positive. On the whole, there is some weak evidence in the elementary and middle school grade spans that choice programs skim off high-scoring students.[3]

---

[2]By "effect" we mean the statistically estimated effect of changing the given variable, holding constant all the other explanatory variables. This effect is not necessarily causal.

[3]This does not necessarily mean that choice programs will result in increased segregation by ability levels, because the integration effects of the programs depend on

For the dichotomous variables, Figure 2.1 shows how much more likely females are to apply relative to males, nonwhites relative to whites, English learners relative to non-EL students, and students with highly educated parents relative to students with less educated parents. Female students in the high school grade span are more likely than their male peers to apply to any of the three programs. However, at the elementary school level, girls are generally no more or less likely than boys to apply to school choice programs, and at the middle school level, a positive effect is seen only for the magnet program. Overall, the findings suggest that if there are benefits to participating in school choice programs, then girls may be as likely as boys to reap those benefits, if not more so. On the other hand, the positive effect of being female on the probability of applying is rather small in comparison with the magnitude of the race and ethnicity variables.

One of the strongest and most consistent results in the analysis presented in this chapter is that black students are much more likely than white students to apply to school choice programs. For example, for the VEEP high school sample, the marginal effect for black students shown on the graph is almost exactly 3.0 percent. By comparison, the overall application rate to VEEP for the high school sample is 3.4 percent, as shown in Table 2.1, which suggests that black students are almost twice as likely as white students to apply to VEEP. The differential between black and white students is not as large for the magnet and open-enrollment programs at the high school level. However, at the middle school and elementary school levels, the differential for the VEEP program disappears. For the magnet program, there are still sizable effects for the middle school grade span, and for the open-enrollment program there are relatively large effects at both the middle school and elementary school grade spans. In all cases blacks are more likely than whites to apply, although the results are not always statistically significant.

There are some similarities between the results for black and Hispanic students. In both cases, the results for high school and middle

the makeup of the sending and receiving schools. Integration issues are addressed explicitly in the next chapter.

21

school grade spans indicate that these students are more likely than whites to apply to choice programs. In contrast, at the elementary school level, there does not seem to be much difference from white application rates. This suggests that of those students who do apply to choice programs, white students are more likely to apply during the early grades, and Hispanic and black students are more likely to apply in higher grades. The results are not as clear for Asian students—sometimes Asians are less likely to apply than whites and sometimes more likely.

In sum, there is little evidence to suggest that nonwhite students are being left out of choice programs and, in fact, the probability of nonwhite applications is particularly high for VEEP. The higher participation rates among nonwhites might also suggest that these students have greater dissatisfaction with their local schools. Another possibility is that white families may have more financial freedom with regard to residential location. (It is also possible that in addition nonwhite families may sometimes face discrimination in housing.) Thus, white families may have less need to make use of choice programs because they are more likely to choose their child's school by choosing where they live.

English learners are usually less likely or equally likely to apply as their non-EL counterparts, looking across all three grade spans and all three programs. One explanation might be that language barriers prevent information about the choice programs from being as well disseminated to non-English-speaking students and parents.

In cases where the findings are statistically significant, our results always indicate that students whose parents have education beyond high school are more likely to apply to school choice programs. However, the magnitudes of the effects are not very large. The findings, taken across grade spans and programs, suggest that school choice programs may lead to a small degree of sorting of students by parental education level. Previous research has found that both parental education levels and the quality of the peer group are linked to student achievement. Sorting by parental education could therefore have important implications for achievement for the students who use the programs and for those in the sending schools and the receiving schools.

Last (as shown in Appendix Tables A.1 through A.3), the higher the grade level, the less likely students are to apply for any of the three choice programs considered in this chapter, although this finding is weaker for VEEP. This general pattern makes sense because students who apply earlier have more years to benefit from switching schools and therefore have a stronger incentive for applying.

What Are Students Looking for in a School?

In addition to the characteristics of the student, the characteristics of the student's local school and those of the schools to which the student is allowed to apply would be expected to affect the likelihood of applying. Figure 2.2 shows the effects of the local school characteristics, and Figure 2.3 shows the effects of the option school characteristics.

Proximity and Distance

To calculate the effects of option school characteristics in a multivariate probit framework, we took an average of the characteristics across all the schools the student could choose from in a given program (VEEP, magnet, or open enrollment), weighting that average by the inverse of the distance-squared to each option school. This method gives more weight to schools closer to the student's home than to those farther away. (Models run using this method were found to perform as well or better than other methods of aggregation that were tested. See Appendix A for details.) We used the location of the local elementary school as a proxy for the student's residence. The elementary school catchment areas are usually one to two miles wide, so that we expect the typical student to live less than one mile from his or her local elementary school.

We tested whether distance to a school matters. Students might be less likely to apply to a school choice program if their local school is close. Conversely, students might be more likely to apply to a choice program if the option school is nearby.

There is some evidence that students are in fact more likely to apply to choice programs if their local school is not close and less likely to apply if the available option schools are distant. For the middle school grade span, Figure 2.2 indicates that students are more likely to apply to either the VEEP or magnet programs if their local school is far away. In the high school grade span, however, distance to the local school does not generally seem to matter much. (We were unable to investigate the effect of local school distance for the elementary school grade span, because we used the local school as a proxy for residence, and so all the students have a measured distance of zero to their local school.)

Figure 2.3 shows that the effect of distance to the option schools on the likelihood of applying to a choice program was found to be negative for the magnet and open-enrollment programs at the elementary school and high school grade spans. At the middle school level, distance seems to have no statistically significant effect on applying to any of the three programs. For the high school sample, there is a statistically significant effect of applying to VEEP but, unexpectedly, the effect is positive. This may be because more distant VEEP high schools also have attractive features not captured in our data and are therefore uncontrolled for. (For example, families may prefer schools that are farther from home if there are problems with drugs, crime, or gang activity in their local area.)

Academic Performance Index

The second school characteristic that we examined was the effect of the school's Academic Performance Index, which is based on the test scores of the students at the school. The API is our primary measure of the academic quality of the school. Information about the API is made available to the public each year by the state Department of Education, so families have access to this information when choosing schools.

Choice proponents have often argued that giving students more options will lead to greater academic achievement throughout a district, because schools improve when they must compete for students. However, if students are not choosing schools on the basis of academic quality, then market forces are unlikely to drive achievement upward. Thus, the influence of academic quality on application behavior becomes important to measure. Because API scores are highly positively correlated with parental education and other measures of socioeconomic status, it is not necessarily the case that a school with high API scores has unusually good teaching, which may be what parents are really seeking. However, the fact that we control for multiple measures of socioeconomic status of the student body at each school increases the probability that what we are measuring with the API is a fair approximation of "school quality."

One might expect that the better the test scores at a local school, the less likely it would be that a student would want to leave that school and apply for a choice option school. Figure 2.2 provides some evidence that supports this hypothesis, but the results are not overwhelming. In most cases, the effect of the local API is not found to be statistically significantly different from 0. However, wherever there is a statistically significant effect, the sign is negative—a higher API at the local school seems to reduce the incentive to apply to choice programs. These results appear primarily for the high school students, indicating that test scores seem to be more important to older students than to younger ones.

One might also expect that students would be more likely to apply to a choice program if the test scores provided through the program schools are higher.[4] Figure 2.3 shows some evidence of such a pattern, but the pattern appears mainly in the high school grade span, and even for high school students, the effect shows up for the VEEP and open-enrollment programs only. The results are further weakened by the fact that elementary school students are actually *less* likely to apply to the open-enrollment program when the average API at the option school is higher than the API at the local school.

Other School Characteristics

The probit models include several other local and option school characteristics: class size, percentage of English learners, percentage of black students, percentage of Asian and Pacific Islander students, percentage of Hispanic students, percentage of students whose parents have education beyond high school, and percentage of teachers holding full credentials.

Figure 2.2 demonstrates that students are generally equally likely or less likely to apply to a choice program when class sizes at their local school are large. This result is somewhat odd; it may arise because large

---

[4]The "Option API dummy" is set equal to one if the average API for the option schools is higher than the API at the local school (see Appendix A for further details on the calculation of the Option API dummy).

class sizes could be negatively correlated with other, more positive school characteristics that we are not controlling for. Figure 2.3 shows quite mixed evidence regarding the effect of class size at option schools. In over half of cases, there is no significant effect, and the remaining four cases are evenly split between a positive and negative effect. In both Figure 2.2 and Figure 2.3, those cases where evidence indicates a preference for smaller class sizes occur at the elementary school level, suggesting that parents value small class sizes more for younger children than they do for older children. Overall, the estimated effects of class size at local and option schools, even when statistically significant, are quite small.

The results provide some evidence that students are less likely to apply for a school choice program when the percentage of English learners at their local school is high (Figure 2.2). This is particularly true for the high school sample, where the result is significant for all three programs. In the section above, on student characteristics, we found that English learners are less likely to apply. There may be a negative networking effect taking place—fewer students at these schools apply to go elsewhere because there are fewer families in the community who have had experience with choice programs, and so information about the programs does not circulate the way it does in the English-speaking community. Alternatively, the negative effect could simply be an artifact of a high degree of collinearity with other variables in the model (issues of collinearity are discussed in more detail in Appendix A). With respect to the effect of the percentage of English learners at the option school (as shown in Figure 2.3), there are no consistent patterns across programs or grade spans.[5]

Regarding the racial and ethnic composition of the student body, the results fail to demonstrate any particularly strong patterns. In general, the higher the percentages of nonwhites at the school (Figure 2.2), the

---

[5]There are some fairly large effects in the middle school grade span, where students are more likely to apply to the magnet program when the magnet schools close to home have a high proportion of English learners; the opposite holds true for the Choice program. Interestingly, this pattern is the reverse of what is seen with respect to the proportion of students who are Hispanic, which is closely correlated with the proportion of students who are English learners.

more likely students appear to opt out of their local school. However, there are several exceptions to this at the high school level. The results are even muddier when it comes to the option school characteristics (Figure 2.3).

In general, students do not appear to have preferences regarding the percentage of their peers who have highly educated parents. The only exception is that parental education levels at the local school do seem to be important to high school students, who are more likely to apply to leave their local school if parental education levels are low.

Mixed results appear regarding the value that students placed on the percentage of fully credentialed teachers at their local school. The strongest result is that for high school students, the probability of applying to the open-enrollment program is less when the percentage of teachers at the option schools who hold full credentials is high (Figure 2.3). This is a counterintuitive result and it is unlikely that it represents the true preferences of the students with respect to credentialing. For one thing, Figure 2.2 shows that the higher the percentage of fully credentialed teachers at the *local* school, the less likely a student is to apply to the open-enrollment program, which would indicate a positive preference for fully credentialed teachers.

Conclusion

The evidence on application patterns presented in this chapter suggests that the fears of school choice critics and the hopes of school choice enthusiasts may both be somewhat exaggerated. Regarding concerns about skimming, there is modest evidence that the school choice programs skim off students with high test scores, students with high grade point averages, students with high parental education levels, and students who are fluent in English. However, as often as not these factors are found to be statistically insignificant as determinants of application behavior.

In addition, the results regarding race may allay concerns that school choice programs are of more benefit to white students than to their nonwhite peers. In fact, the probability of applying is generally higher for nonwhites, with particularly strong effects for blacks. However, we cannot know for certain the effects of the application patterns on integration across the district in terms of achievement, socioeconomic status, or race/ethnicity without comparing the student body composition at the sending and receiving schools. We directly consider the integration question in the next chapter.

Proponents of school choice who believe that increased competition among schools will lead to higher overall achievement levels will not find much support for that position in our analysis. The results indicate that academic criteria such as test scores do not seem to be extremely important to students as they choose schools, making it unlikely that school choice will lead to much competition among schools along this margin, although there are some modest effects seen at the high school level.

3. School Choice and Integration

Both proponents and opponents of school choice in the United States have focused on the potential of school choice to integrate students within a district, not only by race but also by academic achievement levels, parental education levels, and other criteria. Opponents of school choice often argue that the most affluent and well-informed families will take advantage of choice programs by using them to segregate themselves into relatively elite schools. This position stands in stark contrast to the motivating rationale of the civil rights movement of the 1960s and 1970s, which protested the "separate and unequal" nature of America's schools and promoted school choice as an integrative tool. Nationally, the rapid growth of magnet programs and both voluntary and mandatory busing programs in the 1970s resulted directly from court-ordered remedies in education civil rights cases.

San Diego followed this tradition of litigation closely, and today its wealth of school choice programs resembles those of many urban districts across the state and the entire nation. In the 1977 *Carlin v. Board of Education* decision, the California Supreme Court determined that 23 San Diego schools could be considered racially segregated and ordered the district to integrate them. As a result of *Carlin* and other litigation, San Diego implemented a broad range of measures designed to promote racial integration and to provide better opportunities to nonwhite students. Among these were VEEP and the magnet schools, both of which enabled students to choose schools outside their neighborhoods. It was hoped that the resulting transfers would create a balanced racial mix in the district's schools.

After California's passage in 1996 of Proposition 209, which prohibits the use of race as a factor in hiring practices, college admissions, and contracting, VEEP and magnet programs could no longer use a student's race as a factor in granting transfers. Now, any student can apply to attend any magnet school, although students from certain geographic areas receive preference. Similarly, any student can apply to VEEP. As noted above, VEEP schools are grouped into allied patterns, and busing occurs between any pair of schools in the pattern for which the district receives a threshold number of applications. The design of these groupings suggests that typically, but not always, VEEP will continue to integrate the district racially.

In spite of the evolution of VEEP and magnet programs away from the explicit goal of desegregation, in practice these programs today might still act to integrate the district racially and ethnically. The programs provide busing, and both match groups of schools along both socioeconomic and racial/ethnic lines. VEEP does this by grouping together sending and receiving schools with quite different demographic profiles. The magnet program indirectly encourages integration by dividing the district into four clusters and then giving priority to students from the cluster that demographically least resembles the given magnet school over students from other clusters. Those forces are not present in the open-enrollment program. As mentioned above, the open-enrollment option does not provide busing, and so families with their own cars might disproportionately use this program to find better schools for their children. Nor does open enrollment build in preferences for students from certain neighborhoods.

In studying the effect of choice programs on integration, we adopt the approach of the previous chapter by studying applications to VEEP, magnet, and open-enrollment programs for fall 2001. As we hypothesized above, this method provides the clearest picture of the *demand* for school choice. However, in many schools and grades, the number of applications exceeded the school's supply of spaces available. In cases where a lottery was held, we examine how these supply limitations reduced the effect of school choice on integration. Similarly, not all lottery winners chose to leave their local schools, so we study how this further reduction in actual school switching affected integration.

We examine integration first by race/ethnicity, next by average student achievement, then by parental education, and finally by language status. We study how applications, winning applications, and changes in actual school enrollment affected each measure of integration. This analysis is performed overall for all grades and separately for elementary school, middle school, and high school grade spans (for analysis separated by grade span, see Appendix B). We proceed in two stages, first examining how students in each group, whether defined by race/ethnicity, socioeconomic status, or other characteristics, seek to change their peer group by switching schools. This analysis cannot give a "bottom line" as to whether whites and nonwhites increase or decrease contact with each other because, in this case, both whites and nonwhites typically apply to schools with a higher percentage of whites than are attending their local schools. Therefore, the latter part of the chapter calculates the overall change in contact or exposure between the various groups resulting from school choice.

Integration by Race and Ethnicity

Figure 3.1 illustrates the effects of the choice programs on integration between whites and nonwhites at SDUSD. It shows the average difference in the percentage of white students between the choice and local schools of applicants for each racial/ethnic group, based on applications, lottery outcomes, and actual enrollment decisions. (In cases in which a student applied to more than one school in a given program, we took a simple average of the characteristics of the schools applied to. School demographics are calculated from 2000–2001 information.)[1]

One finding shown in Figure 3.1 that applies to all three of the choice programs is that all applicants apply to schools that have a higher percentage of white students. This means that integration caused by nonwhites applying to choice schools with more white students is occurring, but this pattern is somewhat offset by whites who are also choosing to apply to schools with more white students. However, because nonwhites apply in greater numbers than whites, and in higher proportion than their share of the overall student population, on balance

---

[1] Figure 3.1 is a graphical summary of a portion of the results displayed in Table 3.1, which provides a detailed analysis of the effects of all three choice programs on integration across all of the different racial/ethnic groups evaluated in this study. For example, the first bar in the top panel of Figure 3.1 corresponds to the first row and second column of the "Applicant Analysis" portion of Table 3.1. Similarly, the second bar corresponds to the first row and second column of the "Lottery Winner Analysis," and so on.

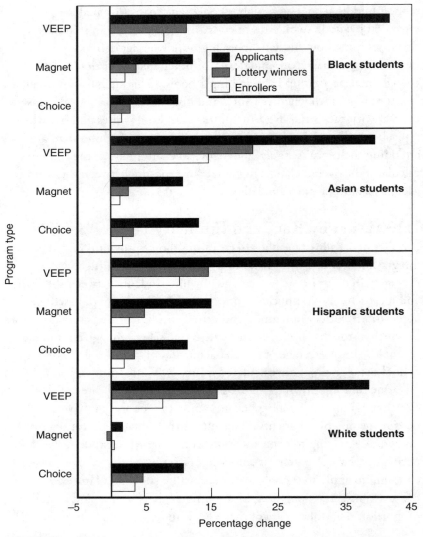

NOTES: The differences shown are those implied by applications, those implied by lottery results, and those based on actual enrollment. Data are aggregated to the district level. The Choice program in this figure refers to the open-enrollment program.

Figure 3.1—Average Differences in the Percentage of White Students
at Option and Local Schools of Program Participants,
by Race and Program Type

Table 3.1

Average Percentage Differences in the Racial/Ethnic Makeup at Option and Local Schools, by Race and Program Type

	Applicant Analysis Student's Own Race					Lottery Winner Analysis Student's Own Race					Actual Enrollment Analysis Student's Own Race				
	White	Black	Asian	Hispanic	Other	White	Black	Asian	Hispanic	Other	White	Black	Asian	Hispanic	Other
VEEP															
% white difference	38.3	41.6	39.6	38.8	44.5	15.6	11.3	21.2	14.6	21.5	7.8	8.0	14.7	10.3	N/A
% black difference	-12.2	-19.4	-11.4	-11.4	-4.1	-6.0	-4.4	-5.8	-4.9	-9.0	-3.7	-3.4	-4.4	-3.8	N/A
% Asian/Pacific Islander difference	-5.9	-5.5	-12.3	0.4	6.1	-2.0	-2.7	-10.5	-0.4	2.0	-2.3	-2.7	-7.9	-0.4	N/A
% Hispanic difference	-21.1	-16.9	-16.8	-28.1	-46.7	-8.2	-4.3	-5.4	-9.6	-15.0	-2.1	-2.0	-2.7	-6.3	N/A
No. of applications	149	710	347	1,696	10	45	154	141	544	1	20	79	88	309	0
Magnet															
% white difference	1.4	12.4	10.9	14.8	9.2	-0.9	3.9	2.6	5.3	4.8	0.2	2.2	1.4	3.0	5.3
% black difference	5.6	-3.6	-1.6	-2.0	2.1	2.6	-2.1	-1.5	-1.4	-1.3	0.9	-1.4	-1.0	-1.5	-2.2
% Asian/Pacific Islander difference	-3.8	-3.9	-6.4	-2.4	-4.6	-1.5	-0.6	-1.6	-1.3	-3.7	-1.0	-0.7	-0.8	-1.0	-4.5
% Hispanic difference	-4.1	-5.5	-3.6	-11.3	-7.4	-0.6	-1.5	0.3	-3.0	-0.1	-0.3	-0.3	0.2	-0.7	1.0
No. of applications	897	1,512	520	1,634	45	379	482	212	590	16	148	189	139	242	10
Choice															
% white difference	10.8	10.2	13.4	11.3	8.9	4.5	2.8	3.7	3.6	5.1	3.3	1.7	2.0	2.0	4.1
% black difference	-3.0	-5.4	-2.9	-3.0	-3.2	-1.9	-1.6	-1.6	-1.7	-3.5	-1.3	-0.7	-0.8	-1.0	-2.8
% Asian/Pacific Islander difference	-1.6	-3.5	-4.8	-2.9	-0.3	-0.7	-1.1	-0.7	-0.7	0.1	-0.3	-0.6	-0.3	-0.4	0.0
% Hispanic difference	-6.5	-1.4	-5.9	-5.5	-5.9	-2.1	-0.2	-1.6	-1.3	-2.2	-1.7	-0.3	-0.9	-0.7	-1.7
No. of applications	1,486	881	620	1,355	46	501	138	133	300	19	323	85	91	167	16

NOTES: The differences shown are those implied by applications, lottery results, and actual enrollment. Data are aggregated to the district level. The Choice program in this table refers to the open-enrollment program.

all three of the choice programs are increasing integration between whites and nonwhites.

The percentage increase of white students from applicants' local schools to their choice schools is especially high for VEEP (for applicants of all races). Because of this, and because applicants to VEEP are mostly nonwhite, the analysis of applications to VEEP indicates that the program plays a large role in integrating whites and nonwhites in the district. Also noteworthy is the fact that within VEEP, elementary school applicants in particular apply to schools that are much more "white" than are their local schools (see Appendix Table B.1).

Of particular relevance for the debate on how deeply school choice might affect racial/ethnic integration is the open-enrollment program, because in this program any student can apply to any school in the district, except for magnet schools. Of the three programs, this in some sense is closest to an unregulated market. Across all racial/ethnic groups, there is a clear pattern showing that applicants are using the open-enrollment Choice program to apply to schools with a higher percentage of white students than in their local school. Furthermore, the application patterns do not suggest that there will be increased mixing among *nonwhite* ethnicities. However, the fact that most applications are made by nonwhites, coupled with the fact that applications from all racial and ethnic groups tend to be made to schools with relatively high percentages of students who are white, suggests that, overall, the open-enrollment program will increase racial/ethnic integration between whites and nonwhites.

The application data from the school choice programs at SDUSD show that students have used the programs in a bid to attend schools that are "more white." However, not all applications are accepted because in many cases the number of applications exceeds the number of spaces available. Figure 3.1 compares the changes in the percentage of white students in applicants' schools, assuming that all applicants win the lottery and actually switch schools, with the changes that are actually possible after adjusting for applications that "lost" in the district's random drawing process. To adjust our calculations for lottery outcomes, we include all students who apply to a given school choice program but set the change in the racial mix they would experience to zero in any cases where all of their applications to a given program (VEEP, magnet, or open enrollment) lost in the lottery process. Therefore, we expect to see smaller changes in the implied racial/ethnic mix because of the enforcement of these supply constraints.

In Figure 3.1, the first bar shows the changes that would result if all applicants won their lotteries. In fact, many applications are randomly rejected because of the limited number of spaces available in the most popular schools. The second bar in each trio of bars in Figure 3.1 shows the changes in racial/ethnic mixing that would occur if only winning applicants changed schools. It shows that supply constraints in the choice programs limit student mobility and decrease the implied average changes in the racial/ethnic mix experienced by the applicant group. For example, the upper panel of Figure 3.1 shows that, if all were accepted, black applicants to VEEP would experience an average change in the percentage of white students at their schools, should they actually switch schools, of 41.6 percent.[2] However, VEEP's actual supply constraint reduces the average implied change in the percentage of white students at the schools of these applicants by 30.3 percent, down to only 11.3 percent. Because many of the applications are rejected, the average outcome experienced by the original group of applicants differs sharply from what the application data alone would suggest.

In some cases, a focus on lottery winners rather than on all applications results in a directional change in the implied integrating effect of a given program. For example, white applicants to the magnet program appear, weakly, to apply to schools that are "more white." However, when we focus on lottery winners, we see that constraints based on program availability actually favor white students applying to schools that are "less white." Therefore, Figure 3.1 shows that white lottery winners tend to win placement into schools that marginally *reduce*

---

[2]Implicitly, this reported counterfactual requires that the resident student populations at the choice schools would not respond to such an inflow of students. Indeed, it seems unlikely that if all applications were declared winners, the resident student populations would not react. Nationally, research suggests that resident students might indeed react. For example, Fairlie and Resch (2002) provide some evidence that white students tend to "flee" to private schools in areas with large numbers of disadvantaged nonwhite students in public schools.

their exposure to other white students, on average. In this specific case, then, competition for scarce slots actually reduces segregation between whites and nonwhites.

Finally, not all lottery winners accept their offer to switch schools. The third bar in each trio of bars in Figure 3.1 depicts *actual* changes in racial/ethnic integration that result from school-switching relative to the changes implied by application and lottery-winner data. In this case, we set the change in the racial mix experienced by applicants to zero in any cases where they did not enroll in a school for a given choice program, regardless of lottery success. Focusing on those who actually enroll should result in a reduction of the implied change in the racial/ethnic mix compared to the lottery winner analysis because not all lottery winners actually choose to attend.[3] Indeed, Figure 3.1 shows that the integrating effects of the choice programs are lower than those implied by both the application data and the lottery-winner data when conditioning on students who actually enroll in the schools to which they applied.

Integration by Student Achievement

Different schools in the San Diego district, like those in large districts all around the country, differ drastically in the achievement levels of their students. If families use school choice as a way to improve the environment of achievement of their children, then we should see clear signs of such improvement when we compare test scores at the sending and receiving schools of choice applicants.

To assess this hypothesis, we use test-score data from the Stanford 9 standardized test for the academic year 2000–2001.[4] We standardize test scores within each grade so that the median student—that is, the student who ranks 50th out of 100, has a test score of zero. We compare

---

[3]It is also possible that conditioning on enrollment would magnify the changes in racial/ethnic makeup implied by the lottery-winner conditional data. This would be the case if the students who choose not to enroll are those who win lotteries at schools where the racial/ethnic differences between their choice school and their local school are in the opposite direction of the group as a whole. However, in our analysis, this does not appear to be the case.

[4]For this analysis, we focus only on applicants who have taken the Stanford 9 standardized test.

the mean percentage difference in the number of students performing above the median at the local and option schools. Again, we extend our analysis to look at lottery winners and students who actually enroll.

Figure 3.2 shows the average difference in the percentage of students whose test scores are above the median between applicants' option and local schools based on applications, lottery outcomes, and actual enrollment. (Again, in cases where a student applied to more than one school in a given program, we took a simple average of the characteristics of the schools applied to.) Across all programs and looking at both above- and below-median performers, Figure 3.2 shows that students use the choice programs to apply to schools where there is a greater proportion of above-median performers. The differences between the

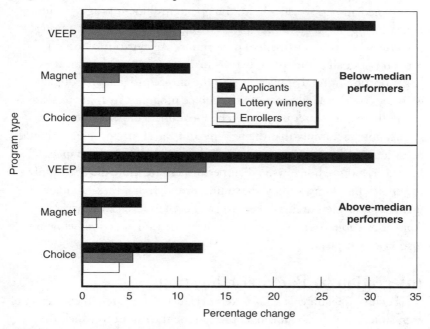

NOTES: See the notes to Figure 3.1.

Figure 3.2—Average Differences in the Percentage of Above-Median Test-Score Performers at Option and Local Schools of Program Participants, by Students' Own Level of Achievement and Program Type

option and local schools are the largest for both student types in VEEP. When we instead focus on lottery winners and then on those who actually change schools, the average magnitudes of the program effects decline, broadly mirroring the results presented for race and ethnicity. This change in magnitudes highlights the value of our methodology as a way to show the gap between the demand for school choice and the supply of slots in receiving schools.

Because we divided students into two groups based on median test scores, we can use the number of applications by student test-score group to determine whether low-scoring students are more or less likely to apply to a given program. For VEEP and magnet programs, the demand for choice appears to be strongest among students who are themselves below-median performers. With the open-enrollment program, the converse appears to be the case, with demand being strongest among students who are above-median performers. Aggregating across all programs and all grade spans, below-median performers constitute a larger portion of total applications to the choice programs. Coupled with the fact that applicants use the choice programs to apply to schools where there is a greater proportion of above-median performers, the application data imply that the net effect of the choice programs should be to increase integration based on student test-score performance. However, although below-median performers are more likely to apply to the choice programs, supply constraints are such that these same below-median performers are less likely to be chosen as lottery winners (see Appendix Table B.4). We return to this issue in the section below on districtwide exposure.

Integration by Parental Education

Each year California schools report data on the parental education of each student. We use these data to examine the extent to which the school choice programs affect the degree of integration by designating three different levels of parental education to facilitate comparison. We will refer to students whose parents have not attended school beyond high school as having "low parental education" and students whose parents have attended at least some college as having "high parental education." Additionally, there is a sizable group of students in SDUSD for which we do not have parental education data. We classify these students as having "unknown parental education."[5]

Following the same methodology as the preceding analysis, Figure 3.3 shows the mean percentage difference in the level of parental education between the option and local schools of applicants, based on applications, lottery outcomes, and actual enrollment. In all programs, applicants apply to schools where a higher percentage of the students have more educated parents. VEEP again shows the largest implied changes for applicants of all parental education types.

The trend encountered previously in the racial/ethnic and test-score analyses is again present when we condition on lottery results and on actual enrollment—the effects of the choice programs implied by the application data alone are dampened considerably.[6]

Integration by Language Status

Closely related to, but distinct from, our race/ethnicity and parental education measures is the percentage of students at a school who are known officially as English learners. In this section, we consider the role of the available choice programs in integrating students who are and are not fluent in English.

Figure 3.4 shows the mean percentage difference between the option and local schools of applicants in the number of students who are fluent in English, based on applications, lottery outcomes, and actual enrollment. In all cases, students apply to schools that have a lower

---

[5]Among elementary school students, the "unknown parental education" group is particularly large because students do not participate in the districtwide testing system from which the parental education data are obtained until the second grade.

[6]It is interesting to note that for high school students whose parents are designated as having high parental education, supply constraints in the magnet program create the only instance where lottery winners were in effect steered toward schools with lower socioeconomic status. That is, in this case applicants in the high parental education group who won the lottery were on average offered magnet schools that had lower percentages of students whose parents were designated as having high parental education than at the applicants' local schools (see Appendix Tables B.10 and B.11). This provides a rare instance of supply constraints working to integrate the schools, running against the more general finding throughout this chapter that supply constraints reduce the extent of integration.

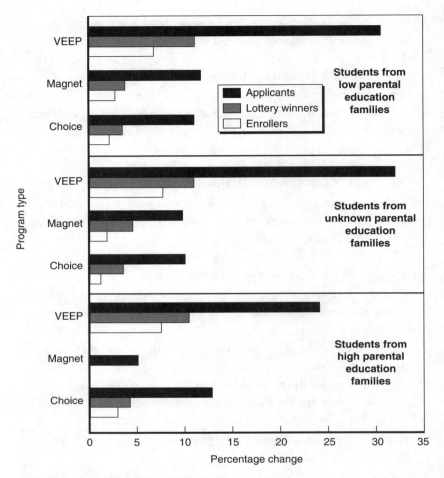

NOTES: See the notes to Figure 3.1.

Figure 3.3—Average Differences in the Percentage of Students from High
Parental Education Families at Option and Local Schools of Program
Participants, by Students' Own Parental Education
Designation and Program Type

proportion of English learners. The differences between the choice and
local schools of applicants are again the largest in VEEP. Furthermore,
the differences between the option and local schools are also larger for
the magnet program than they are for the open-enrollment program. Of

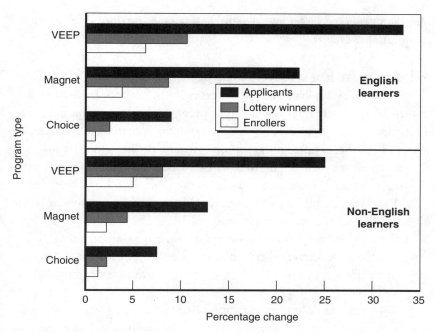

NOTES: See the notes to Figure 3.1.

Figure 3.4—Average Differences in the Percentage of Non-English Learners at Option and Local Schools of Program Participants, by Students' Own English-Learner Status and Program Type

note, the implied changes in the percentage of students who are English learners in the choice schools relative to applicants' local schools are particularly large at the elementary school level for both VEEP and magnet programs (see Appendix Table B.13).

Figure 3.4 shows the familiar reductions in the magnitudes of the effects implied by the application data after adjusting first for lottery outcomes and then for students who actually enroll. For all programs and for both English learners and English-fluent students, the mean percentage difference in the number of students who are not English learners between option and local schools is *always* positive. When conditioning on lottery winners and then on students who enroll, VEEP unambiguously generates the largest average difference between the choice and local schools of applicants. Furthermore, the magnet program generates larger average differences than the open-enrollment program does.

Changes in Districtwide Exposure

The detailed analysis above is informative but cannot by itself give information on whether school choice programs lead to greater or lesser integration districtwide. We therefore extend our analysis to the overall effect of the three choice programs on districtwide intergroup exposure in San Diego schools. To do this, we use what social scientists refer to as exposure indices. For example, we divide students into English learners and those who are fluent in English. For the typical fluent student in the district, we find the average proportion of EL students in his or her school and, conversely, for EL students, the average proportion of English-fluent students at their schools. These proportions are what exposure indices measure. The formula for such an index is provided in Appendix B.

Of course, we do not expect applications for a single year to change markedly the exposure of one group of students to another. It is the sum of many years of applications and subsequent school switches that determines how the overall mix of students changes. However, we use this snapshot of one year's worth of school moves because for this subset of school choice participants, we know exactly where they would have gone to school if they had not enrolled in any of the choice programs. This allows for the accurate calculation of the counterfactual.

Figure 3.5 shows districtwide changes in exposure for each of our four measures of integration. In each case, we show the net change in exposure resulting from the combination of all programs and the change in exposure attributable to each program individually. For clarity of exposition, Figure 3.5 shows our results for exposure to the group that is implicitly the most sought-after in each case. Data tables that provide information on all of our exposure-indices calculations are available in Appendix B (Appendix Tables B.16 through B.19).

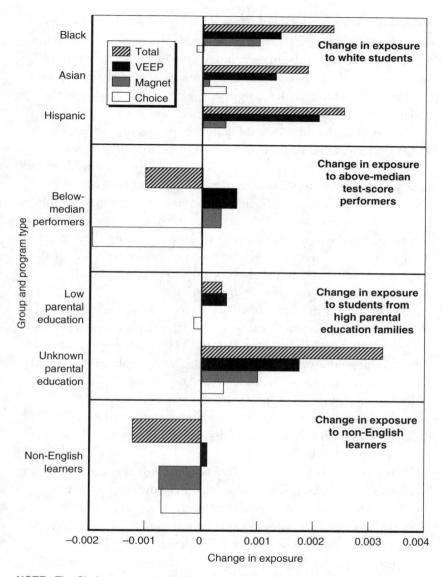

NOTE: The Choice program in this figure refers to the open-enrollment program.

Figure 3.5—Changes in Actual Exposure Generated by the Choice Programs

Not surprisingly, the results from Figure 3.5 show that VEEP has the strongest integrating effects across all measures of diversity used in this study, followed by the magnet program (which integrates along all dimensions except language status). In contrast, the open-enrollment Choice program generally has a *segregating* effect, most notably in the student-achievement and language-status analyses.

Focusing on the top panel of Figure 3.5, we can see that racially, VEEP and magnet programs unambiguously increase the exposure of whites to nonwhites, and vice versa. (We can add the exposure of whites to each of the other groups to infer changes in exposure of whites to nonwhites.) The open-enrollment program increases the exposure of whites to Asians but decreases the exposure of whites to blacks and Hispanics. Of the three programs, VEEP by a wide margin exerts the strongest influence over changes in white to nonwhite exposure for all nonwhite groups. The overall effect of the choice programs is to integrate whites and nonwhites in the district.

Similarly, the net effect of the choice programs on the exposure of Hispanics to non-Hispanics is also positive (this result is largely driven by integration between Hispanics and whites). However, the net effects of the choice programs on the exposure of blacks to nonblacks and Asians to non-Asians are negative. Although the choice programs integrate whites and nonwhites, they have a net segregating effect on the exposure of nonwhite students to each other. In fact, the effect of each of the choice programs on the exposure of nonwhite students to each other is negative (see Appendix Table B.16).

The next panel of Figure 3.5 shows districtwide changes in exposure based on student achievement. It paints quite a different picture from the analysis based on race. Dominated by the negative effect of the open-enrollment Choice program, the overall consequence of choice programs on integration by student achievement is negative.

Next, the parental education exposure indices show that the choice programs in the district increase the exposure of students from low or unknown parental education families to those designated as being from high parental education families. However, this analysis is clouded by the ambiguity surrounding the "unknown parental education" group. As can be clearly seen in Figure 3.5, integration between parental-education groups consists mostly of integration between students designated as being from high parental education families and students whose parental education status is unknown. Looking specifically at the overall change in exposure between students from high and low parental education families, the effect of the choice programs seems quite mild.

Finally, our language-status exposure indices show that the net effect of the three choice programs (dominated by the magnet and open-enrollment programs) is a clear decrease in the exposure of English learners to non-English learners. Again, VEEP still results in a small increase in EL to non-EL exposure when taken alone, but this effect is overcome by the negative changes in exposure created by the other two programs.

Part of the explanation for the negative effect on exposure between EL and non EL-students lies in the program participation rates of EL students. English learners in SDUSD in 2000–2001 made up 27.4 percent of the student population. Application data show that the only program in which EL applications exceeded the EL share of the student population in 2000–2001 was VEEP, which had a net positive effect on the exposure of EL and non-EL students to each other. In both the magnet and open-enrollment programs, EL students were largely underrepresented as applicants. Because all applicants use choice programs to reduce their exposure to English learners, it is not surprising that the lack of participation of EL students themselves in these programs reduces their exposure to non-EL students overall.

Conclusion

Overall, students (and their families) use choice programs to improve the socioeconomic status of their school environment. With regard to race, this means that applicants use the choice programs as vehicles to attend schools that are "more white." This does not necessarily mean that families explicitly make decisions based on race, because race is correlated with many other closely entwined factors. For instance, applicants also appear to use these programs to attend schools that have a higher proportion of above-median test-score achievers, more students who have highly educated parents, and fewer students who are English learners.

Because the majority of applicants to the various choice programs are nonwhite, these programs tend to increase integration between whites and nonwhites within the district. As a by-product of applicants' attempts to attend schools that are "more white," the net effects of the choice programs on integration among nonwhite racial/ethnic groups are negative.

Across all of the choice programs and all grade spans in SDUSD, the demand for choice exceeds supply. Therefore, the extent to which students are able to use these programs to alter their school-level peer groups is limited by accessibility. By focusing on the original applicant group for each level of our analysis (race, student achievement, parental education, and English-learner status), we examined the extent to which supply-side constraints limit the intended changes in the school-level peers of applicants. In all cases, we find that supply-side constraints do indeed limit the average magnitude of the changes intended by applicants and in most cases these constraints have a rather large limiting effect.

In addition to the supply shortages created by the lottery process itself, lottery winners who choose not to change schools also limit the effect of changes in the socioeconomic environment at option schools. Although it is unclear exactly why not all lottery winners choose to attend their option school, some simply leave the district. It is interesting to note that among the lottery winners who do not attend their choice school the following year, just 4.2 percent of VEEP winners and 7.3 percent of magnet winners fail to do so because they have left the district. However, in the open-enrollment program, 21.0 percent of winners who did not accept the offer left the district. For the remaining groups, their motives for not attending their choice school are unknown.

To the extent that program applicants consist of students of low socioeconomic status attempting to integrate with students of high socioeconomic status, the limiting effects of the supply constraints ultimately reduce the level of integration achieved by the various programs. For example, along racial and ethnic lines, supply-side constraints do appear to limit the net level of integration within the district. However, this is not always the case. Our analysis of integration by English-learner status shows that supply-side constraints ultimately serve to stave off attempts of non-EL students to further *segregate* themselves from EL students.

Finally, our analysis examines the extent to which the choice programs in the district affect actual districtwide integration, considering only applicants who actually enroll in the various programs. Our findings indicate that the choice programs ultimately increase the exposure of whites to nonwhites and decrease the exposure of nonwhites to other nonwhites. Similarly, the choice programs increase the exposure of students whose parents are relatively more educated to students whose parents are relatively less educated. The aggregate effects of the choice programs on EL to non-EL exposure and on exposure by student-achievement level are *negative*.

Overall, VEEP and magnet programs appear to increase integration at SDUSD. Furthermore, in most cases and along most dimensions, VEEP has the strongest integrating effect. The Choice open-enrollment program does the least to boost integration, and across some measures of diversity, it actually segregates the district's schools.

We see two explanations for the different effects of the open-enrollment program. First is the lack of busing in that program, which may discourage applications from disadvantaged families. Second, both VEEP and magnet programs have features intended to give priority to exchanges between groups of schools that should increase integration along racial/ethnic and socioeconomic lines. Open enrollment does not give anyone higher priority.

Finally, it is worth noting that the actual moves made by students in fall 2001 to option schools changed the exposure of one type of student to another by quite small amounts. For instance, compare the actual percentage of students who are Hispanic in the average white student's school in fall 2001 to the counterfactual case in which no school switches had been permitted. We find that as a result of the lotteries for fall 2001, districtwide, the exposure of whites to Hispanics increased from 27.3 percent of peers to 27.6 percent of peers. It would be quite wrong to conclude, though, that the *cumulative* effect of school choice lotteries across many years is similarly small. On the contrary, these effects are additive over time and are meaningful.

4. Does School Choice Boost the Achievement of Those Who Win Lotteries?

The central issue for policymakers is whether switching schools through a choice program increases a student's achievement. Because of the use of lotteries in SDUSD, we are in an unusually good position to respond to this question. Traditionally, research on the effects of school choice on achievement has compared students who switch to students who stay behind at local schools or to students at the receiving schools who live in that school's local attendance area. But students in these comparison groups could differ in motivation and in many other ways from students who choose to switch. As outlined in Chapter 1, the great virtue of lotteries is that they produce a valid comparison group of students who lost in the lottery drawing. On average, students who win and lose a given lottery should be identical in terms of initial test scores, socioeconomic background, and unobservable characteristics such as motivation.[1] We can then compare the test scores between these two groups, thereby providing an unbiased or "true" estimate of the effect on student achievement of winning a lottery. If school choice succeeds in the sense that it offers a better education to those who are offered a spot at an option school, we should be able to detect this. Because the district uses lotteries to draw students randomly into the winning and losing groups, our approach is an example of a quasi-experimental research method.

In analyzing the effect of winning a lottery, we have to consider some extremely important details. First, it cannot be assumed that all students

---

[1]Throughout this report, we refer to the selection procedure as being a series of lotteries, and we also refer to lottery winners and losers. District administrators do not use any of these terms, instead referring to the randomization used to admit students. Technically, these are indeed lotteries and we use that language solely to convey in an understandable manner the procedure used for selecting students.

who applied to a given school participated in the same lottery. Rather, within all three programs, separate lotteries are held by grade level at a given school and within a grade level, students are further subdivided into separate lotteries based on a student's priority status. The exact nature of these priority groups differs slightly across programs. We explain this in Appendix C.

After sorting applicants into the schools and grades they applied to and into their respective priority groups, we can thus identify the specific lottery they entered. We exclude some lotteries in which all applicants either lose or win, because these are not true lotteries at all. (In these cases demand for a given school is either very large or very small relative to the supply of slots.) Such situations defeat our goal of comparing lottery winners and losers who differ only in the luck of the draw. We therefore identify "true" lotteries, by which we mean lotteries in which not all students won and not all students lost.

It is one thing to know that a lottery is being conducted and another to verify that the lottery is "fair," in the sense that winners and losers in a given lottery on average had the same test scores in spring 2001, around the time of the lottery. (Test scores and all other personal characteristics should *on average* be the same between winners and losers in a given lottery because the only difference between the two groups is the random numbers they drew.) We examine this question using the entire sample of lottery applicants and find that there was no statistical difference between the two groups in terms of initial test scores. (Appendix C provides more details including a separate test of this proposition for every test-score model presented in this chapter as well as for the additional models in Appendix C itself.)

Our next step is to test whether lottery winners had greater achievement one, two, and three years after winning the lottery. We test this idea using a variety of reading and math tests administered to all students in relevant grades each spring. During the period under study, California required that districts administer two different types of tests to all of its students. The first, the California Standards Test (CST), is a "criterion-referenced" test designed to test students' mastery of the state's content standards in various subjects, grade by grade. The second type of test is a "norm-referenced" test. Rather than setting absolute standards of what students should know, norm-referenced tests compare students to a nationally representative sample. In spring 2002, California used the Stanford 9 test for this purpose and in spring 2003 and 2004 switched to a similar test known as the CAT/6. For all of these tests, we study achievement in math and reading. In addition, the San Diego district administered another norm-referenced test, the Stanford Diagnostic Reading Test (SDRT), to students in grades 4 through 10 throughout our period of study. Overall, then, in most grades we have two measures of math achievement and three measures of reading achievement in each year.

To test whether students who won a lottery fared the same on these tests in years after the lottery as those who lost, we separately model the spring 2002 through spring 2004 test scores of students. In our simplest specification, specification (1), we model test scores as a function of a dummy variable to indicate whether a student had won the lottery, including a set of dummy variables for each lottery that we add to account for the fact that average achievement will differ among lotteries. If winning a lottery has no effect on achievement, then we should find that the coefficient on the dummy for lottery winners should be "statistically insignificant," that is, indistinguishable from zero.

We also estimate a series of more elaborate models:

- In specification (2), we add the spring 2001 test score in the same or the most closely related test in the same subject (math or reading) to the 2002 to 2004 scores.[2] Although on average there should be no difference between winners and losers of a given lottery, in practice there will almost always be some small, presumably random, differences. By controlling for the student's test score at the time of the application lottery, we can increase the precision or reliability of our estimates, because controlling

---

[2]For CST, we use spring 2001 CST test scores, measuring the number of questions correct, as opposed to the scaled scores available in later years. We tested and found that this raw test score in 2001 was actually quite highly correlated with later scaled CST scores. For the Stanford 9 scores in spring 2002 and scores in the replacement for the Stanford 9, the CAT/6, in spring 2003 and 2004, we used spring 2001 Stanford 9 test scores. For the SDRT, we used spring 2001 SDRT scores.

removes any difference in achievement measured in spring 2001, around the time of the lottery.[3]

- In specification (3), we control for the same 2001 test score and also its square, to allow for nonlinear relations between current-year and past test scores.
- In specification (4), we add a host of personal characteristics of each student.
- Finally, in specification (5), we add a fairly rich set of variables describing the student's class size, peer group test scores from the prior year, and teacher characteristics. This model is useful because it tests whether we can explain any effects of winning a lottery in terms of differences in school and classroom characteristics.

We focus mainly on the results of specification (2) below but present the results of all five specifications in Appendix C.

What follows is a list of the explanatory variables used to model reading and math achievement in the years after the 2001 lotteries. The numbers below refer to the specification, with each specification appending the variables in the prior specification:

1. Lottery winner, controls for each grade level, controls for each lottery. A lottery is categorized by the school, grade level, and priority code of each application.
2. Control for 2001 test scores in CST, Stanford 9, or SDRT in the same subject being modeled (reading or math).[4]
3. Control for 2001 test scores, squared values of 2001 test scores.

---

[3]The statistical result that controlling for prior achievement can increase statistical precision substantially in a randomized study has been documented by numerous authors (see, for example, Donner and Klar, 2000; Bloom, 2003).

[4]All test scores used as a dependent or explanatory variable were standardized to a mean of zero and a standard deviation of 1. CLAD is an acronym for the Crosscultural, Language, and Academic Development credential, which prepares teachers to teach students who are English learners. BCLAD, the bilingual CLAD, is similar but prepares bilingual teachers to teach in a bilingual classroom. We include separate controls for alternative language certifications to the CLAD and BCLAD.

4. English-learner status, English-fluent status, redesignation status for that particular year, parental education level, student ethnicity, and student gender.

5. Controls for classroom characteristics, such as class size and peer groups;[5] controls for teacher characteristics, such as credential type, education level, and years of experience; controls for CLAD, BCLAD, CLAD alternative, and BCLAD alternative credential. For these variables of classroom and school traits, averages were taken over a three-year period.

It is worth saying more about why the initial test scores of lottery losers and winners in a given lottery could differ. Even if the original lottery is "fair," differences in initial test scores could appear in the 2002, 2003, or 2004 regression samples because of a systematic difference in who drops out of our samples by spring of these years, one, two, and three years after the lottery. This would be an example of selectivity bias. For each of the regressions shown in Tables 4.1 and 4.2, we test whether there is a statistically significant difference in prelottery test scores in the samples remaining by each of the three years. Only in about 8 percent of cases do we find evidence that these spring 2001 test scores are different at the 5 percent level of significance. Even if there were no true differences, we would expect about 5 percent of cases to show up as significant because of random variation. We are very close to this. (In over two-thirds of these rare cases, the prelottery scores of lottery winners were significantly lower than those for lottery losers; details appear in Appendix Table C.3.) In such instances, we place much greater confidence in specifications (2) and (3) because they do condition on the prelottery test score.

It seems quite likely that school choice could vary across elementary, middle, and high schools in effectiveness at boosting student achievement. The difference in quality of instruction, as well as the ability of students to sustain the daily travel necessitated by school choice, could differ by grade level and students' age. Thus, although we present results that pool all

---

[5]We did not have peer group information for 2001–2002 CST scores because we did not have standardized scores for the prior year. However, we did have peer group data for the 2003–2004 school year. We took the average over all the prior years, except for 2001–2002.

Table 4.1

Estimated Effect of Winning a VEEP, Magnet, or Choice Lottery on Various Measures of Reading Achievement, by Grade Span, Spring 2002 Through Spring 2004

Grade Span	Test Year	Test	VEEP	Magnet	Choice
All grades	2002	CST	−0.0994**	0.0497	0.0215
		Stanford 9	−0.0872*	0.0753*	−0.0173
		SDRT	−0.0839*	0.0299	−0.0172
	2003	CST	−0.0575	0.0602	0.0294
		CAT/6	−0.0595	0.0858	−0.0397
		SDRT	−0.0490	0.0492	−0.0098
	2004	CST	0.0055	0.0578	−0.0319
		CAT/6	−0.0065	0.0031	−0.1036*
		SDRT	−0.0898	0.0295	−0.1915**
Elementary school	2002	CST	0.0645	−0.0259	0.0406
		Stanford 9	0.1301	0.1383	−0.0010
		SDRT		0.1417	−0.0924
	2003	CST	−0.1617	0.0107	−0.0231
		CAT/6	0.4441*	0.1452	−0.1996
		SDRT		0.3170*	−0.1318
	2004	CST	0.5353*	−0.0949	−0.1639
		CAT/6	0.2512	−0.0779	−0.3013**
		SDRT		0.1088	−0.6047**
Middle school	2002	CST	−0.0868*	0.0094	−0.0010
		Stanford 9	−0.0678	0.0034	−0.0319
		SDRT	−0.0980*	−0.0305	−0.0544
	2003	CST	−0.0157	−0.0173	−0.0212
		CAT/6	−0.0628	−0.0149	0.0273
		SDRT	−0.0605	−0.0228	−0.1042
	2004	CST	−0.0222	0.0399	−0.0521
		CAT/6	−0.0384	−0.0612	0.0012
		SDRT	−0.0902	0.0181	−0.1426*
High school	2002	CST	−0.1915*	0.0893	0.0032
		Stanford 9	−0.1839*	0.0683	0.0410
		SDRT	0.0050	0.0327	0.0851
	2003	CST	−0.1081	0.0978	0.0129
		CAT/6	−0.1262	0.0854	−0.1075
		SDRT	−0.1262	0.0620	0.1459*

Table 4.1 (continued)

Grade Span	Test Year	Test	VEEP	Magnet	Choice
	2004	CST	0.0844	0.0261	0.0370
		CAT/6	0.0043	0.0269	−0.1111
		SDRT			

NOTES: Each cell refers to the coefficient for the dummy indicating that the student won the given lottery. Each regression models the test score (with mean zero and standard deviation 1 districtwide, for each grade and year) as a function of the dummy for having won a lottery, the student's 2001 test score, fixed effects for the specific lottery, and a random effect for the actual school attended. Appendix Tables C.4 through C.9 provide coefficients for this and four other specifications, and include the above models as specification (2). Also, a web appendix available at http://www.ppic.org/content/other/806JBR_web_only_appendix.pdf provides full regression results.

*Significantly different from zero at the 5 percent level.

**Significantly different from zero at the 1 percent level.

available grades for a given test, we also show results estimated separately for the three grade spans.

Results

To give the reader a bird's-eye view of the results, Figures 4.1 and 4.2 present results for the CST in reading and math, respectively, based on specification (2), which models test scores one, two, and three years after the spring 2001 lottery as a function of each student's grade level and initial test score in 2001. Each of these figures shows three separate graphs for VEEP, magnet, and open-enrollment Choice lotteries. The bars in each graph show the sample size available for the regression model; the sample size can be read off the left-hand axis of each graph. It is important to show this because in a few cases we have relatively small samples, in which case we are quite likely to find a "zero" effect even if, in reality, winning the given lottery increases or decreases the average winning student's subsequent achievement. The cross-shaped figures in each graph show the estimated effect of winning a lottery as well as the 95 percent confidence interval for this estimate. The horizontal line on the cross shows the estimated effect, and the vertical line shows the 95 percent confidence interval. The latter shows the possible range of the actual

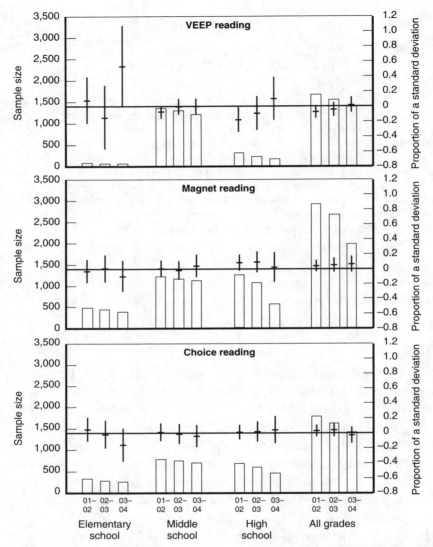

NOTES: In the graphs, the horizontal line on each "cross" shows the estimated effect of winning a school choice lottery, measured in standard deviations; the corresponding vertical line shows the 95 percent confidence interval. The bars show the sample sizes used in the underlying regression and the scale for this is found on the left-hand side of each graph.

Figure 4.1—Models of the Effects of Winning School Choice Lotteries on CST Reading Achievement: Effect Sizes, Confidence Intervals, and Regression Sample Sizes

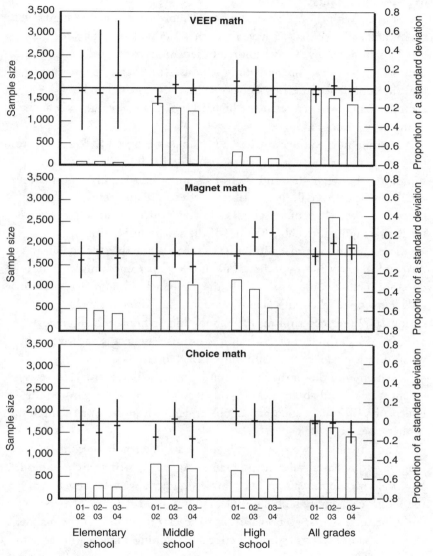

NOTE: See the notes to Figure 4.1.

Figure 4.2—Models of the Effects of Winning School Choice Lotteries on CST Math
Achievement: Effect Sizes, Confidence Intervals, and Regression Sample Sizes

effect of winning a lottery, with a 95 percent chance that the true value lies within this range.

Starting with the VEEP reading results in the top panel of Figure 4.1, we immediately see that we have more than 1,000 observations for the middle school model, a few hundred observations for high schools, and only 45 observations for elementary schools. It is therefore not surprising that the confidence intervals are very small for the middle school estimates, somewhat larger at the high school, and really quite big at the elementary school level.

Turning next to the estimated effects of winning a VEEP lottery, from the right-hand scale we see that most of the estimated effects are somewhere between –0.1 and +0.1 of a standard deviation and usually are much smaller. Overall, these estimated effects are quite small. The exception is the elementary school estimates, which we already know are likely to be quite unreliable because of the small sample size.

The standard approach in statistics is to assume that the actual effect is zero and to reject this hypothesis only if the 95 percent confidence interval does not include zero. As shown in the top panel of Figure 4.1, there are only a few cases where this "confidence interval" does not include zero: spring 2002 test scores for middle school, high school, and all grades samples. In all three of these cases, the estimated effect is negative. Thus, we find little evidence that winning a VEEP lottery boosts reading achievement and that it may temporarily lower achievement. However, we must be careful about making conclusions of any sort regarding the effects of VEEP on elementary school students given the small sample size in that case.

The remaining two panels in Figure 4.1 show reading results for magnet and open-enrollment programs. Again, elementary school models have the fewest observations but sample sizes are always far larger than for the VEEP elementary school sample, ranging from 320 for the open-enrollment elementary school sample to several thousand for the magnet all grades sample. The estimated effects of winning a magnet lottery on reading achievement are very small and they are never statistically significant. (Note that the 95 percent intervals always include the possibility of a zero effect.) Similarly, for the open-enrollment program, we again find small effects that are not significantly different from zero.

The overall pattern continues to hold with regard to math results, as shown in Figure 4.2: Typically the effect of winning a lottery is not significantly different from zero. But there are some important exceptions. Perhaps most important for policy, the results suggest that winning a magnet lottery at the high school level is associated with positive gains in math achievement two and three years later. As shown in the middle panel of Figure 4.2, the size of the effects is meaningful in a policy sense, at roughly 0.2 of a standard deviation in test scores. Also, in middle schools, winning either the VEEP or open-enrollment lotteries is associated with slightly lower math achievement in 2001–2002, one year after the lottery. However, in later years the effect becomes insignificantly different from zero.

What about results for tests other than the CST? Tables 4.1 and 4.2 summarize results for each of the tests available to us.[6] Each entry shows the estimated effect of winning a lottery on student achievement. Because we standardized all of our test scores to have mean zero and standard deviation 1 within each grade, these coefficients can be interpreted as the number of standard deviations by which lottery winners move above or below lottery losers by the year stated. It is important to assess these coefficients in the context of statistically significant results, denoted by asterisks. Coefficients without an asterisk are not significantly different from zero, whereas there is a probability of only 5 percent and 1 percent, respectively, that coefficients with one or two asterisks are truly zero. Thus, the conservative way to read these tables is to treat only the significant coefficients as being different from zero.

Table 4.1 shows our estimates for reading. Each entry in this table shows the coefficient for lottery winners for a specific school choice program, grade span, year, type of reading test, and specification. For instance, the coefficient on the top line of the table refers to a regression for the VEEP sample that included all grades for the CST test in 2002. The coefficient is negative and statistically significant, and suggests that

---

[6]These tables, like Figures 4.1 and 4.2, use specification (2), which models test scores as a function of initial (spring 2001) test scores, lottery dummies, and the key variable indicating whether the person won the lottery. Appendix Tables C.4 through C.9 summarize our results for all specifications. There, each table shows the results for one of the three school choice programs and one of the two subject areas, math and reading.

one year after the lottery, winners had CST reading scores about 0.1 of a standard deviation below lottery losers.[7] This coefficient corresponds to the results shown for VEEP in this case in Figure 4.1. Below this entry, we also show results for the Stanford 9 and SDRT reading tests.

The broad patterns in these results are as follows: There is some evidence that students who win a VEEP lottery have lower reading achievement than lottery losers one year after the lottery, with this effect limited mainly to middle schools and perhaps high schools. Two and three years after the lottery, we see differences in reading achievement that are almost always statistically insignificant.[8] Table 4.1 shows that the CST results shown in Figure 4.1 are matched quite closely by models of the alternative measures of reading prowess, such as the Stanford 9.

One result suggests that CST reading scores for elementary school students who won a VEEP lottery become significantly higher by year 3. However, this is based on a very small sample and it should probably not be given a lot of weight.

In sum, VEEP lottery winners and losers typically fared about the same in reading. The main exception is that CST scores in 2002 may have been about 0.1 to 0.2 standard deviations lower for lottery winners in middle and high schools.

Table 4.2 shows corresponding VEEP results for math. Here, we find little evidence that VEEP lottery winners and losers achieved at different levels in math relative to each other in any of the three years. The only exception is CST math scores in middle school, where achievement is

---

[7]Appendix C reproduces all of these results and, for interested readers, shows in addition standard errors, sample sizes, the number and percentage of observations pertaining to lottery winners, and the number and percentage of observations representing lottery winners who actually transferred to the school to which they had applied or to a higher grade span school in the same feeder pattern as the school to which they had applied, by the given year.

[8]There are two exceptions. In spring 2003, two years after the lottery, middle school winners appear to be faring worse on the CAT/6 but only in specification (1), which does not condition on prelottery test scores. Conversely, elementary school winners seem to outperform losers on the CAT/6 in spring 2003. But this occurs in only one of the five specifications. Moreover, the elementary school sample is quite small and therefore we do not place much confidence in this finding.

Table 4.2

Estimated Effect of Winning a VEEP, Magnet, or Choice Lottery on Various Measures of Math Achievement, by Grade Span, Spring 2002 Through Spring 2004

Grade Span	Test Year	Test	VEEP	Magnet	Choice
All grades	2002	CST	−0.0730	−0.0192	−0.0247
		Stanford 9	−0.0257	−0.0362	−0.0438
	2003	CST	0.0197	0.1235*	−0.0175
		CAT/6	−0.0063	0.0234	−0.0380
	2004	CST	−0.0304	0.0661	−0.1078
		CAT/6	0.0184	0.0990	−0.0516
Elementary school	2002	CST	−0.0378	−0.0717	−0.0472
		Stanford 9	0.0449	−0.1317	−0.0126
	2003	CST	−0.0648	0.0128	−0.1247
		CAT/6	0.2194	0.0886	−0.0120
	2004	CST	0.1289	−0.0460	−0.0522
		CAT/6	0.1566	−0.0098	−0.0542
Middle school	2002	CST	−0.1035*	−0.0270	−0.1678**
		Stanford 9	−0.0327	−0.0165	−0.0694
	2003	CST	0.0247	0.0133	0.0208
		CAT/6	−0.0156	−0.0652	−0.0706
	2004	CST	−0.0336	−0.1359	−0.1864
		CAT/6	−0.0073	0.0353	−0.0730
High school	2002	CST	0.0695	−0.0255	0.1021
		Stanford 9	0.0011	−0.0277	−0.0014
	2003	CST	−0.0204	0.1824*	0.0033
		CAT/6	−0.0055	0.0155	−0.0400
	2004	CST	−0.0296	0.2308*	−0.0110
		CAT/6	0.1008	0.0849	−0.0696

NOTE: See the notes to Table 4.1.

about 0.1 of a standard deviation lower for lottery winners than for lottery losers in 2002. However, this difference disappears in later years.

The Magnet column of Tables 4.1 and 4.2 shows our results from the magnet lotteries, for reading and math achievement, respectively.

Winners of magnet lotteries generally have reading scores that were statistically indistinguishable from the scores of those who lost the lotteries one to three years after the lottery was held. For math achievement, this general trend is repeated, except at the high school level.

In these high school regressions, we see perhaps the strongest regression results in this chapter. We find no significant differences in 2002, but in both 2003 and 2004, math CST scores are about 0.2 of a standard deviation higher for magnet lottery winners than for losers. The estimated effect is slightly larger in 2004 than in 2003. CAT/6 math scores show a positive gap as well, but these are not statistically significant.[9]

The final column of Tables 4.1 and 4.2 shows corresponding results for the open-enrollment Choice program. The first set of rows, which shows results that pool across all grades, suggests no effect from winning an open-enrollment lottery except that two different reading tests indicate that by 2004, three years later, lottery winners had reading scores 0.1 to 0.2 standard deviations below those of lottery losers. When we examine the separate results by grade span, we see that this negative result in 2004 appears to derive from both elementary and middle schools, with the former showing quite a large negative effect of −0.3 to −0.6 of a standard deviation. In contrast, we find some evidence of a positive effect of winning a lottery in high schools in 2003. However, as shown in Appendix Table C.8, this single positive result is not robust: The effect disappears when we include personal traits in specification (4).

The final column of Table 4.2 shows math results for open-enrollment lottery participants. With one exception, we find no statistically significant effect of winning a lottery. In middle schools in 2002, lottery winners scored below lottery losers on the CST. However, even here, the test for identical prelottery test scores suggests that in this sample, prelottery test scores were lower for lottery winners. Further, in specification (4), where we add a host of personal characteristics, this effect disappears, as shown in Appendix Table C.9. This variation in results

---

[9]It is possible that the CST, which is tied to California's quite rigorous high school content standards in math, does a better job of discerning mastery of this material than does the standardized CAT/6 test.

suggests that personal differences between the lottery and winners could account for any differences in the test scores, rather than the program itself.

Overall reading results for the open-enrollment program suggest for the most part no effect from winning a lottery, except for some negative outcomes in 2004 in elementary school and, to a lesser extent, middle school. Similarly, the math results suggest that the most conservative and careful conclusion we can make about the Choice program is that overall there is no strong evidence that lottery winners performed better or worse in math than lottery losers in the three succeeding years.

Thus far, we have treated school choice as something of a black box, focusing on the overall effect of choice on achievement without inquiring into mechanisms. One general question we would like to ask about all forms of school choice is: If winning a lottery affects achievement, what is the reason? This question is largely moot given that most typically, we have found no significant effects to explain. But what about the isolated cases in which winning a lottery is associated with significantly different achievement in later years? For instance, can we explain the positive effect of winning a magnet school lottery on high school math scores in terms of class size or the qualifications of the student's math teacher? In Appendix C we present results for specification (5) to test whether any significant differences in outcomes between lottery winners and losers could be explained by factors such as class size, teacher qualifications, and other school and classroom characteristics.

In general we found that these variables had little explanatory power. This fact is perhaps best seen in the high school results for magnets. If these classroom and school factors account for the higher test scores of lottery winners in 2003 and 2004, then we should see the coefficient on lottery winners becoming smaller in specification (5) than in specification (4). However, the opposite result appears. This implies that whatever it was about the magnet program that appears to have boosted math achievement in high schools is not easily captured by the standard measures of school and classroom characteristics.

Conclusion

Our results are quite complex and subtle, but overall, lottery winners and lottery losers typically have no significant differences in math or reading achievement one, two, or three years after the lottery takes place. What are the main exceptions? First, high school magnet programs are associated with higher math achievement for lottery winners two and three years after the lottery. These differences are meaningful, at about 0.2 of a standard deviation in test scores. Second, we found scattered evidence for each of the three programs that one year after the lottery, winners sometimes had significantly lower test scores than losers. However, these differences appeared to be temporary in that they were no longer apparent two and three years after the lottery. This pattern suggests that switching schools can create temporary adjustment costs for students. As our next chapter on charter schools will discuss, the literature on charter schools has sometimes found similar effects.

In interpreting these results, it is important to clarify what our research design can and cannot accomplish. First, the lottery application basis provides a compelling framework by which to evaluate the overall effect of winning a lottery. Unlike traditional studies that compare students who choose to leave with those who stay in their local schools, we have a comparison group of students who, like the lottery winners, had the same motivation to leave their local schools. However, by the luck of the draw, they were not granted admission. Because this is the only difference between the lottery winners and losers, any differences in subsequent outcomes should be attributable to whether the student won or lost the given lottery. In practice, it is possible for small differences to emerge, because of either natural randomness or nonrandom attrition of students from the sample as the years pass by. We verified that in 92 percent of cases, our regression samples exhibited no difference in *average* 2001 (prelottery) test scores. For the remaining cases, we tend to prefer the models that control for prelottery achievement. In fact, it has long been established that controlling for initial achievement can greatly increase the precision of estimates, even in the absence of selectivity bias.

Also, note that we are estimating only the effect of winning a lottery—not the effect of winning and subsequently attending the school.

The former question is of legitimate policy interest: If a superintendent orders that an additional 1,000 offers go out, what is the expected gain in student achievement districtwide? Our approach can help to answer that question. Appendix C discusses some of the technical reasons why we are hesitant to attempt to estimate the actual effect of winning a lottery and switching schools.

Although there are great strengths in this quasi-experimental design, it is important to consider how these results can and cannot be used. Because all of the students in our samples applied to leave their current schools, they likely differ in important ways from students who did not apply. Therefore, we cannot use these results to infer what would happen in a world in which *all* students were forced to exercise their right to choose a school. (There are additional problems with extrapolating to a world of universal choice: The number of "nonlocal" students at a given school would presumably be much higher, and this could alter many aspects of the school including curriculum scheduling, the mix of teachers who choose to teach at that school, and the nature of peer-group interactions among students. In particular, with more widespread school choice it is possible that many local students might flee from some receiving schools, that is, begin to attend school elsewhere, possibly in the private school system.)

On a related note, because we used only "true" lotteries in which some but not all students win the lottery, we exclude students who applied to the most and least popular lotteries. This might tilt our sample toward the most popular schools, although for the most part we found ourselves ignoring lotteries where everybody in the given priority group at a given school and grade was admitted, in favor of the priority group further down the list. In spite of these qualifications, our results suggest that, with the important exception of high school magnets, overall lottery winners progressed in math and reading at about the same rate as lottery losers. This result does not square easily with the evidence in earlier chapters that these choice programs are very popular: Each of the three programs attracts roughly 5 percent of students in the district, and available spaces serve only a fraction of the demand.

There are two possible explanations. The first is that parents are not fully informed about differences in the quality of education provided in different schools. The second is that even if parents value math and reading achievement, they place their children in nonlocal schools for reasons apart from achievement. This explanation seems particularly plausible for the magnet school program, which provides specialized programs in a range of areas, including creative and performing arts, language immersion, English, math, and science and technology. It is therefore somewhat intriguing that it is the magnet program, with its diverse goals, that appears to show the strongest evidence of boosting math achievement.

Do the mixed results in this chapter suggest that school choice is "not working" in San Diego? Although our results raise some important questions, it would be premature to make sweeping conclusions about public school choice based on outcomes for one set of students who entered lotteries to switch schools in fall 2001. Outcomes could have differed somewhat in other years. Also, even with the second largest school district in California, we do have a limited sample size—if we had had more data, then effects that are statistically insignificant in our results could conceivably have become statistically significant. This is especially the case for the VEEP elementary school regressions, where our sample size was quite small. At the same time, it is important to recognize that our estimated effects on achievement, even if typically insignificant in a statistical sense, are typically also small in a policy sense. For instance, in our pooled regressions across all grades, we typically find estimated effects of winning a lottery of around 0.05 or 0.1 of a standard deviation, even after allowing three years to pass before assessing outcomes for lottery winners and losers. These effects would appear meaningful if they were both statistically significant and had accrued in a single year; after three years, effects of this size are too small to do much to boost achievement in a way that would alter the test-score gap between high-achieving and low-achieving students.

Indeed, the apparently small effects of choice raise major questions about the reliance of the federal NCLB law on school choice as a primary way to eliminate the achievement gap. We return to this issue in the concluding chapter.

5. A Portrait of Charter Schools and Their Effect on Student Achievement

Charter schools are publicly funded but free from many of the regulations governing traditional public schools. These schools represent a vital component of the overall choice program available to SDUSD students and are possibly the most emblematic features of the broad movement in education reform that emphasizes choice and competition. The underlying principle of this movement is that if parents and students are given opportunities to leave failing schools, all schools will be forced to improve to attract and retain students.

As shown in Figure 5.1, charter schools have increased their share of overall SDUSD enrollment steadily since 1997. They are divided into two types, conversion and startup. Conversion charter schools are standard public schools that change their relationship to the district, often retaining teachers and serving the same student population at the same school site but no longer bound by district regulations governing standard schools. Startup charter schools are entirely new. These schools secure facilities unaffiliated with the district and independently recruit new classes of students and teachers when they open.

Federal NCLB legislation requires that districts restructure schools that fail to attain state adequate yearly progress standards for six years. One possible way to restructure is to convert the school into a charter school. Many schools have already begun to do this. In San Diego in fall 2005, three large district schools were required to restructure, reopening as conversion charter schools. The federal law puts new pressure on districts nationwide to create conversion charters out of existing public schools, so public policymakers may wish to treat startups and conversions differently. We analyze their performance separately.

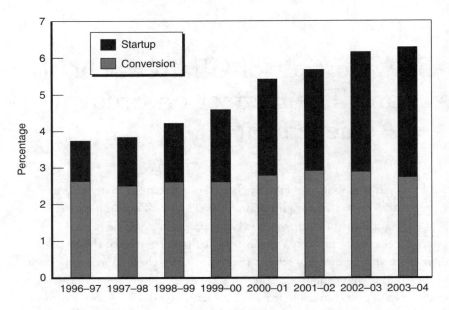

Figure 5.1—Charter School Enrollment Growth in San Diego Unified School District Schools (% of district students enrolled in charter schools)

Background

Charter schools in San Diego date back to the 1993–1994 school year. The earliest charter schools tended to be conversion schools. Four of the five longest-operating charter schools in San Diego are conversion schools. The two elementary schools among these opened during a period in which there was overcrowding at several elementary schools in the district. During this period, a few individuals in the community were interested in creating new schools with educational programs and operating procedures different from those offered by the district. In part to alleviate the overcrowding pressures and in part to satisfy community demand for new alternatives, the district authorized two new schools to operate on two separate elementary school campuses that had previously been closed. One of these was already open before the state charter legislation passed and only afterward became classified as a charter school. The two conversion middle schools were both district middle schools with special curricula already in place before the passage of state charter legislation. After the passage of the legislation, both of these schools applied for charter status to gain more freedom from state and district regulations, becoming conversion charter schools. The remaining one of those five oldest schools, the Charter School of San Diego, is classified as a startup but originated as a district program serving middle and high school students determined to be at high risk of dropping out.

Most of the recent growth in San Diego's charter school enrollment has been in startup schools. Figure 5.1 shows that although conversion school enrollment has been relatively constant through 2004, the percentage of charter school students who attend startups has risen markedly. However, this trend is changing with the recent conversion of several schools, noted above, and may change further with the hiring of a new district superintendent and changes in school board membership in 2005.

Although SDUSD has clearly embraced the charter movement, as evidenced by the rapid increase in enrollment percentage, charter schools in San Diego have faced the same challenges as others in California and the nation. Foremost among these are financial. Charter schools appear to be less well funded than regular public schools. The reasons are complex, but two common problems relate to facilities and busing. Most charter schools lease space from nondistrict landlords, and these costs typically are paid from public funds based on each school's average daily attendance (ADA). Noncharter schools use these same ADA funds to pay staff and related costs. Betts, Goldhaber, and Rosenstock (2005) cite evidence that in California, the costs of renting private space could eat up 20 or even 30 percent of a charter school's revenues; charters that are able to lease unused district buildings typically pay something closer to 3 percent of revenues for rent. (Such discrepancies have resulted in litigation in San Diego. In December 2005, the California Charter School Association and two local charter schools sued the district because the two schools had been denied unused space in existing district school buildings. The lawsuit claimed that this practice was a contravention of state laws that guarantee charter schools access to unused space in existing district school buildings.)

Another major but less common problem (at least in San Diego) involves the cost of busing. Across the nation, some charters that draw from an unusually wide geographic area must pay for busing or subsidies for public transportation out of ADA funding. Regular public schools do not bear this cost. Again, the result is less funding per student available for the classroom.[1]

Unlike VEEP and open enrollment, charter schools are *school-based* rather than *student-based*. That is, the entire student population has elected to attend a given charter school, whereas at option schools participating in the three other types of school choice, only a small percentage of students has elected to attend. This distinction makes it important to study the overall characteristics of charter schools themselves.

We begin by comparing charters to regular public schools in terms of student demographics, teacher characteristics, and class sizes. We also summarize results from a survey of charter school senior administrators in San Diego. Although our assessment reveals that charter schools share many traits, such as a strong academic focus, the charter school program as a whole in San Diego is surprisingly diverse in its goals and teaching methods.

Second, we undertake a statistical analysis of the effect of attending a charter school on student achievement in reading and math. Because there is no centralized lottery for charter school applications, we compare the gains in achievement of individual students in years they attend charters to their gains in years they do not attend charters. This so-called student fixed-effect model eliminates the need to compare students at charters with those who do not attend charters. Such comparisons of

---

[1]The Preuss School, a charter school on the University of California, San Diego (UCSD) campus that aims to prepare students from relatively disadvantaged backgrounds for college, provides a useful case in point. Virtually none of the students lives close to UCSD, and so the school's students depend heavily on busing. During the initial charter period, from 1999 through 2004, the district that granted the charter, SDUSD, agreed to pay for busing. But when SDUSD renewed the Preuss School's charter in 2004, it rescinded the busing subsidy. Fortunately, the Preuss School was able to lease school buses from the district, but it had to pay for this out of its regular funds. This new cost amounted to about 7 percent of its 2004 funding. By way of disclosure, we note that Julian Betts, coauthor of the present report, has served on the Board of Directors of the Preuss School since 1999 at the request of the university's chancellor.

different students could have proven unreliable if there were unobserved differences between students who choose charters and those who do not. Instead, by comparing each student's achievement gains when in and out of the charter program, we in effect use each student as his or her own comparison group.

Researchers employing this method have recently completed studies of charter schools in Texas, Arizona, Florida, and North Carolina. In Arizona, charter schools appear to improve student reading achievement, and student math performance is comparable to that in regular public schools (Solmon, Paark, and Garcia, 2001). Sass (2006) finds that in Florida after an initial startup phase where charter schools face difficulties, performance is on par with regular schools. This is a similar result to that of Hanushek et al. (2005) studying schools in Texas. However, charter school performance in North Carolina appears to be worse than regular public schools, even after the initial startup period (Bifulco and Ladd, 2006). These sometimes contradictory results highlight the need for more research into charter schools in various contexts and in more detail.

A Comparison of Students, Teachers, and Class Sizes

Although for charter schools we lack the centralized application and lottery data that proved so helpful in Chapter 3, we can learn much about charter schools and racial/ethnic integration by comparing their student mix with that of regular public schools. Table 5.1 illustrates that charters and regular public schools have different racial mixes. Hispanic and black students constitute disproportionately more of the charter sector than they do of the district as a whole, whereas white and Asian students constitute disproportionately less. The overrepresentation of Hispanic students in the charter sector is even more striking in the conversion charter schools.

In the 2002–2003 school year, Hispanic students accounted for 41 percent of district enrollment, 48 percent of charter enrollment, and 62 percent of students in conversion charter schools. Notably, startup charter schools have a slightly smaller share of Hispanic students

Table 5.1

Enrollment by Race and Meal Assistance Eligibility, San Diego Unified School District Schools, 2002–2003

	Overall District	Regular Public	Charter	Charter Startup	Charter Conversion
% Hispanic	40.88	40.39	48.23	35.62	61.85
% white	26.16	26.77	17.19	28.14	5.38
% Asian	17.44	17.79	12.25	9.06	15.70
% black	15.00	14.53	21.89	26.64	16.77
% American Indian/other	0.52	0.52	0.43	0.54	0.30
	100	100	100	100	100
Total number of students	140,753	131,865	8,888	4,613	4,275
Number of schools	185	165	20	16	4
% eligible for free meals	45.96	45.22	56.87	40.26	74.81
% eligible for free or reduced-price meals	56.63	56.02	65.68	49.90	82.71

SOURCE: National Center for Education Statistics, 2002–2003.

NOTE: Numbers may not sum to 100 percent because of rounding.

than regular public schools do as a whole. In contrast, black students appear to be disproportionately attending startup charter schools. Nearly one-quarter of startup charter students are black, whereas blacks make up only 15 percent of the district as a whole. White students are underrepresented in conversion charters, and Asian students are underrepresented in startup charters. The table also reveals that students in charter schools tend to be more socioeconomically disadvantaged than their regular public school counterparts when measured by eligibility for free or reduced-price meals. This result is driven by conversion charter schools, where nearly three-quarters of students qualify for free meals. At startup schools, a slightly smaller percentage of students than in the district as a whole qualify for subsidized meals.

Another way to look at charters is through test scores. Table 5.2 shows average API scores for regular schools and charter schools by year. Charters have tended to lag behind but do catch up significantly over time. This later convergence may be related to the large growth in the number of startup charter schools, which tend to have higher API scores

Table 5.2

Academic Performance Index Averages, 1999–2004

	1999	2000	2001	2002	2003	2004
Regular public schools	646	694	685	693	717	735
Charter schools	558	630	646	648	691	718
Startups	531	646	685	672	718	740
Conversions	571	599	568	527	629	659
Difference						
Regular – charter	89	64	39	45	26	17
Number of regular school						
scores	157	142	157	158	161	156
Number of charter school						
scores	6	9	12	12	19	20
Number of startup school						
scores	2	6	8	10	15	16
Number of conversion						
school scores	4	3	4	2	4	4

SOURCE: http://api.cde.ca.gov/datafiles.asp.

than conversion charters. The bottom lines in the table show the number of schools of each type in each year contributing to the averages displayed in the upper part of the table.[2] These average test scores tell us little about the relative quality of charter and regular schools, because students' initial academic achievement before coming to charter schools may be higher or lower than the districtwide average. The API scores provide only snapshots of average student performance that may not be related to school influence.

Tables 5.3 and 5.4 summarize the results for teacher characteristics and class size, comparing charters with regular public schools and conversion with startup charter schools, respectively. We first summarize the differences in observable teacher characteristics between charter and traditional public schools, and startup and conversion charter schools. Table 5.3 separately displays characteristics by grade span of schools so that we do not inadvertently attribute differences resulting from different

---

[2]This is not the entire sample of district schools. A small number of schools do not have APIs in some years because of insufficient data or testing irregularities.

Table 5.3

Teacher Characteristics, 1997–1998 to 2003–2004

	Noncharters	Charters	Conversions	Startups
Overall				
Age	43.700	38.700**	39.800	35.500**
Years of service	14.600	8.900**	9.800	6.400**
Years of service in SDUSD	12.100	6.000**	6.700	3.700**
Salary	48,910	42,536**	42,580	42,206
Master's degree	0.576	0.365**	0.368	0.344*
Ph.D.	0.009	0.013	0.009	0.034
Full credential	0.966	0.936**	0.944	0.899**
Intern credential	0.014	0.013**	0.113	0.101
Emergency credential	0.031	0.114**	0.096	0.193**
Teachers in Elementary Schools				
Age	42.200	38.500**	40.300	36.700**
Years of service	12.900	7.400**	8.100	6.700**
Years of service in SDUSD	10.600	4.500**	5.400	3.700**
Salary	46,257	38,803**	38,715	38,993
Master's degree	0.526	0.341**	0.364	0.297
Ph.D.	0.004	0.000	0.000	0.000
Full credential	0.931	0.821**	0.871	0.764**
Intern credential	0.034	0.020	0.009	0.033
Emergency credential	0.030	0.252**	0.198	0.313**
Teachers in Middle Schools				
Age	42.900	39.600**	39.700	33.100**
Years of service	13.700	9.700**	9.900	4.000**
Years of service in SDUSD	11.100	6.700**	6.800	2.300**
Salary	48,243	42,802**		
Master's degree	0.547	0.368**	0.369	0.000
Ph.D.	0.006	0.009	0.009	0.000
Full credential	0.980	0.947**	0.948	0.711**
Intern credential	0.008	0.013*	0.013	0.000
Emergency credential	0.037	0.092**	0.090	0.289*
Teachers in High Schools				
Age	44.700	35.300**		
Years of service	15.600	6.000**		
Years of service in SDUSD	13.100	3.500**		
Salary	50,332	41,473**		
Master's degree	0.605	0.352**		

Table 5.3 (continued)

	Noncharters	Charters	Conversions	Startups
Ph.D.	0.011	0.023		
Full credential	0.969	0.910**		
Intern credential	0.011	0.006		
Emergency credential	0.026	0.184**		

NOTES: No information is available on salaries for teachers in conversions and startups at the middle school level. There are no conversion schools in San Diego at the high school level.

*Noncharters vs. charters, or conversions vs. startups, are statistically different at the 5 percent level.

**Noncharters vs. charters, or conversions vs. startups, are statistically different at the 1 percent level.

grade spans served to differences in actual characteristics between the sectors.[3]

Charter school teachers are younger and less experienced, both in total years of service and in years with the school district, than traditional public school teachers. Because teacher salaries are determined in large part by experience, average charter school teacher salaries are also correspondingly lower. Fewer charter school teachers have master's degrees than do traditional public school teachers. Charter school teachers are less likely to hold full credentials and much more likely to hold emergency credentials.

The difference in teacher experience is even more startling when examining startup charter schools. Although the average charter school teacher has about six years of district experience, approximately half the average of 12 years of a noncharter teacher, the average startup school teacher has even less experience—less than one-third the district experience of the noncharter teacher. In the traditional public school sector, high school teachers tend to have more experience than elementary and middle school teachers, so the difference in experience between charters and noncharters is especially pronounced at this level. Charter school teachers at middle or high schools appear to be somewhat

---

[3]Teachers who teach in schools serving a combination of grade spans are included in each grade span, since we do not know which grades the teacher teaches.

Table 5.4

Class Sizes, 1997–1998 to 2003–2004

	Noncharters	Charters	Conversion	Startup
Overall				
Overall (including special education)	26.24	27.48**	27.13	28.58**
Overall (excluding special education)	27.78	27.85	27.54	28.82**
Overall (special education only)	10.08	11.13*	11.91	4.38**
Elementary Schools				
Overall	20.62	20.34	20.79	19.92*
Nonspecial education	21.68	20.73**	21.21	20.28*
Special education	9.03	6.00*	7.09	4.67
Middle Schools				
Overall	28.63	27.53**	27.60	25.17**
English classes	27.11	25.54**	25.56	24.79
Math classes	29.02	27.86**	27.89	26.79
Other academic classes	30.00	27.34**	27.40	25.60
Nonacademic classes	34.52	31.06**	31.32	23.57**
Special education	10.25	12.32**		
High Schools				
Overall	27.65	32.91**		
English classes	26.75	27.58		
Math classes	29.34	27.11**		
Other academic classes	30.38	29.46		
Nonacademic classes	31.20	38.79**		
Special education	10.60	4.00*		

NOTES: There are no conversion schools in San Diego at the high school level. Academic classes include foreign languages, science, and social sciences. Nonacademic classes include art, dance, drama/theater, health education, music, physical education, and Special Designated Subjects (e.g., driver education).

*Noncharters vs. charters, or conversions vs. startups, are statistically different at the 5 percent level.

**Noncharters vs. charters, or conversions vs. startups, are statistically different at the 1 percent level.

more likely than their regular school counterparts to have doctorates, although this difference is not statistically significant.

Table 5.4 shows that overall, charter schools have slightly larger class sizes than traditional schools. However, once special education classes are excluded, the difference becomes statistically insignificant because special education classes tend to be smaller and charter schools have fewer of them.[4] At the elementary school level there is not much difference in class size between the types of schools. At the middle school level, charter schools seem to have somewhat smaller class sizes in every category except special education. Startup middle schools have especially small class sizes. At the high school level, charter classes appear larger overall, but this effect is driven by large nonacademic classes. High school charters actually have significantly smaller math classes statistically. All of these high school charters are startups; there are no conversion high schools in San Diego.

To summarize, teachers in charter schools tend to be younger, less experienced, and less likely to have master's degrees or full credentials. Charters and noncharters appear to have similar class sizes overall, although charter schools appear to have smaller academic class sizes. These differences between teacher and classroom characteristics are more evident when comparing startups to traditional schools than when comparing conversion charters to traditional schools, because conversion charters are qualitatively closer to traditional public schools.

Now that we have provided an initial comparison of charter and noncharter schools based on centrally collected administrative data, we explore differences within charter schools as revealed in survey data.

Survey-Based Evidence on San Diego's Charter Schools

In June 2004, we distributed a survey to the 21 charter schools operating under the oversight of the district. Five schools declined to participate in the survey, leaving 16 responses.[5] The responses show a surprising amount of heterogeneity in charter school operations. Charter schools indeed appear to be exercising their freedom from rules

---

[4]In 2000–2001, 3.07 percent of noncharter students and 0.56 percent of charter students were classified as special education.

[5]The five charter schools that did not return the survey are from the lower end of the San Diego charter school distribution as measured by the API. This does not necessarily mean that the nonresponding schools offer a lower-quality education, although it does suggest that these schools likely serve underperforming students.

governing traditional public schools and to be implementing policies different from those of traditional public schools and from each other.

Table 5.5 presents means and standard deviations for many of the survey responses. Although space constraints prevent us from running through every element in this table, we present main patterns below.

Students Served

Rather than focusing on just one of the traditional levels—elementary, middle, or high school—we note that many charter schools offer a combination of the traditional levels—either elementary and middle, or middle and high. Around one-third of the schools in our sample serve a combination of levels, and these are about evenly split between grades K–8 and 6–12 or 7–12. Of the 14 schools that serve students at more traditional levels, eight are elementary schools, four are middle schools, and two are high schools. Conversion charter schools tend to have larger student populations than startups do. At the middle school level, the two conversions averaged 1,400 students and the startups averaged only 200. The difference is less dramatic at the elementary school level, where the two conversions average 400 students and the six startups average 200.

Charter schools differ greatly in the percentage of students residing in the local attendance area, with conversion schools typically reporting higher numbers. Notably, half of the responding schools (and three-quarters of startups) report that less than 30 percent of their student population live in the local attendance area. This implies that many charter schools draw students from a broad area and that they therefore do not resemble traditional neighborhood schools along this one important dimension. Five schools do appear to be more like traditional public schools with more than 70 percent of their students coming from the local attendance area. At one of these schools, a conversion, all of the students reside in the local area. The three remaining schools report that between 41 and 60 percent of students reside in the local area, an almost even mix of neighborhood and nonneighborhood students.

Five of the schools target students living in a particular area within San Diego, but only one of these is located in that same area (with more than 70% of students living there). The four others are either located far

Table 5.5

Summary Statistics of Responses to Charter School Survey, June 2004

	All Charters		Conversions		Startups	
	Mean	Std. Dev.	Mean	Std. Dev.	Mean	Std. Dev.
From Administrative Data						
Average daily attendance	429.4	433.4	926.0	610.7	263.9	186.8
Year of operation	5.5	3.3	10.0	0.8	4.0	2.3
Elementary school	0.625	0.500	0.50	0.577	0.667	0.492
Middle school	0.500	0.516	0.75	0.50C	0.417	0.515
High school	0.125	0.342	0		0.167	0.389
Facilities						
Operates in church/religious building	0.4375	0.512	0	0	0.583	0.515
Operates in traditional school building	0.3125	0.479	1	0	0.083	0.289
Operates in office space	0.250	0.447	0	0	0.333	0.492
Students						
Target students	0.533	0.516	0	0	0.727	0.467
Target particular area	0.313	0.479	0	0	0.417	0.515
Target disadvantaged	0.500	0.516	0	0	0.667	0.492
Target limited-English-proficient	0.313	0.479	0	0	0.417	0.515
Target at-risk students	0.125	0.342	0	0	0.167	0.389
Proportion of students residing in local attendance area	0.397	0.337	0.683	0.271	0.302	0.309
Operations						
Longer school day	0.500	0.516	0	0	0.667	0.492
Longer school year	0.250	0.447	0.25	0.5	0.250	0.452
Number of instruction days	182.3	7.8	180	0	183.1	9.1
School has a wait list	0.813	0.403	0.75	0.5	0.833	0.389
School conducts random lottery for admission	0.500	0.516	0	0	0.667	0.492
Teachers subject to collective bargaining agreement	0.188	0.403	0.75	0.5	0	0
Proportion of teachers from the district	0.224	0.259	0.438	0.423	0.153	0.145
Parent Involvement						
Number of mandated parent-teacher meetings	0.667	0.488	0.5	0.577	0.727	0.467
Number of parent-teacher meetings	3.188	2.762	3.75	3.594	3	2.594

Table 5.5 (continued)

	Mean	Std. Dev.	Mean	Std. Dev.	Mean	Std. Dev.
Mandated parent volunteer hours	13.500	24.478	6.667	11.547	15.364	27.101
Parent volunteer hours	35.917	33.560	35.5	48.790	36	33.347
Parents must sign learning contract	0.438	0.512	0.75	0.5	0.333	0.492
Challenges Facing the School[a]						
Finances are a problem	2.813	0.403	2.75	0.5	2.833	0.389
Facilities are a problem	2.750	0.447	2.75	0.5	2.75	0.452
Parental involvement is a problem	2.625	0.500	2.5	0.577	2.667	0.492

[a] 3 = major problem; 2 = minor problem; 1 = not a problem.

away from most of their students or draw students from a broader area than they target.

Half of the schools in our sample report that they target disadvantaged students, and of those eight, five in particular target students classified as English learners. Among the eight schools targeting disadvantaged students, two explicitly seek students whose parents have not finished college.

Although nine of the schools answered yes to the question of whether there is an application process for admission to the school, only two responded with the particular criteria used to determine admission. One of these schools demands parental commitment to contribute 54 hours of volunteer work to the school a year; the other uses parent education and socioeconomic status along with past academic records and scores on tests administered by the state or district to determine eligibility for the admission lottery. It is important to note that these schools are looking for disadvantaged students who would be the first from their families to attend college. Seven schools conduct interviews and gather letters from teachers that describe students' progress, past academic records, or scores on tests administered by the state or district. In all but one of these schools, however, this information is used not for admission decisions but only to assess academic levels and to gain knowledge of the student body before the first day of school.

The most popular student recruitment strategy appears to be word-of-mouth. Some schools post flyers in the neighborhood and advertise in community newspapers or newsletters. Other recruitment efforts include direct mailings to students or schools, public school visits, and special recruitment events. Charter schools appear to be quite popular. Only three of the schools returning the survey did not have a wait list. Of those three, one is not a typical public school—it serves only kindergartners and first graders in close association with Head Start, a preschool program. Another was surveyed in its first year of operation.

In the district as a whole, it appears that students and parents are quite interested in exploring the charter school option, regardless of the specific type of school.

School Focus, Curriculum, and Operating Policies

As described above, many of the schools target low-income and socioeconomically disadvantaged students. Five schools report that they target English learners, and another six offer an emphasis on a specific language or culture. The majority of these offer Spanish bilingual programs, but there are also schools emphasizing German, black history, and Harambee (school unity). Other characteristics described by principals as focuses of their schools include collaboration, interdisciplinary approaches, project-based learning, adult world connections and service-learning, lifelong learning, creative thinking, individual needs, focus on teachers, college-prep, arts, technology, and California's state educational standards that set guidelines on what students should know by each grade. Several schools also offer music or sports/physical education programs as special features.

In regard to specific policies, about half the charter schools offer a longer school day than traditional public schools do. Several of these start the school year earlier or eliminate the once-a-week half day often found in traditional schools. Three of the schools instruct students late into the day, educating students until 4 or 5 p.m. Whereas only four of the schools report a longer school year (one of these operates on a year-round calendar), the number of instructional days varies quite a bit, ranging from 175 to 200, with an average of 182.

We also asked charters what specific resources they make available for students identified as "below basic" on the California state achievement tests. Fourteen schools offer before/after-school tutoring for these students, and three schools offer Saturday classes. Four schools offer supplementary services under NCLB, one more than those that offer services under the state's Immediate Intervention/Underperforming Schools Program (II/USP)—an intervention program in which schools work with an outside consultant to improve student achievement. Two schools offer both programs. Other interventions noted were in-school day "safety nets," one-on-one tutoring in school, intersession and summer school sessions, and association with a private clinic for children with learning difficulties.

Facilities and Financing

Five (about 30%) of the schools operate in traditional school buildings. Four of these five are the conversion schools whose facilities are owned by the district; the remaining one is a college-prep middle and high school located on the campus of the University of California, San Diego, in a building constructed with privately donated funds. Seven schools lease or borrow space from a church or a synagogue, with the remaining four schools operating in unused government or office buildings. Although conversion charters are all located on district property, they do not share the same relationship to the district.[6]

Subsidized transportation for students is arranged for five of the schools—two of these are conversion elementary schools. The other three report that less than 20 percent of students reside in the local attendance area. Two of the schools offered district-paid and district-provided busing in the past, but neither does now, because of the expiration of a federal grant in one case and in the other, a judgment by the district that it could no longer pay for busing. The latter school still offers busing but funds the busing internally and through donations.

---

[6]Three of the conversion schools are declared as arm-of-the-district schools, with the remaining operating as a 501(c)(3) nonprofit. The district's charter schools are about evenly split between those operating as nonprofits and those operating as arm-of-the-district charters. The former have greater autonomy.

We asked principals to rate the challenges facing the school. "Finances" is the category most schools seem to view as a "major problem." Ten schools cite this as a "major problem," and another four view it as a "minor problem." Even schools receiving relatively large one-time grants seem to view annual operating expenses as a problem. All schools received some outside grants, but the size of these grants differs enormously. We asked schools to approximate the amount of outside funding they received in previous years and in the most recent school year; the number reported ranges from $17,000 to $800,000. Schools appear to use very different funding sources. Five schools reported that private donations from parents are a primary source of funding, and nine received money from businesses or foundations. Eight schools use government grants, which are either competitive or created by State of California legislation aimed at charter schools in general. All schools have some formal partnerships with community organizations, businesses, learning centers, or local colleges and universities. The governing boards of the charter schools differ considerably, although most have a mixture of parents, teachers, and community members. The conversion middle schools have many more teachers on their boards than the other schools do.

Teachers

Only three of the schools (all of them conversions) report that their teachers are subject to the district's collective bargaining agreements, but an additional six report that wages for teachers are set according to or similarly to the district salary schedule. The percentage of teachers coming from the San Diego Unified School District ranges from 0 to 95 percent, with conversion schools typically having more teachers from a traditional public school in the district. When considering startup schools only, the maximum is only 50 percent. The average percentage of teachers coming directly from the district is 22 percent overall: 44 percent in conversion schools and 15 percent in startup schools.

Parental Involvement

Charter schools employ many different strategies to involve parents. Most schools have parent organizations, and the number of times a year the organization meets ranges from four to 18. Six schools require that parents volunteer their time and in these schools, the required amount of volunteer time ranges from 15 to 80 hours a year. The amount of time a parent of a typical student actually volunteers (including at schools in which it is not mandatory) ranges from one to 70 hours a year. Schools that formally required that parents volunteer for relatively more hours appear indeed to elicit more parent volunteer hours, although it is not possible to determine whether there is a causal relationship. Parents volunteer most at elementary schools.

There seems to be a significant range of activity in the forms and levels of parental involvement within charter schools. Six schools do not view lack of parental involvement as a problem at all, but four view it as a major problem and six as a minor problem. The conversion schools all report that lack of parental involvement is a problem. Ten schools make individual parent-teacher conferences mandatory. Most schools hold these individual meetings to discuss student progress between one and three times a year, but teachers at two schools meet individual parents more than eight times a year. Seven schools require that parents sign a learning contract. None of the schools that view parental involvement as a problem requires mandatory meetings between teachers and parents. It is important to note that this does not necessarily suggest that mandating meetings would increase parental involvement; it may be the case that the underlying lack of parental involvement renders mandatory meetings ineffective.

As noted above, the oldest charter schools in the district are conversion charters and these tend to be larger than startups. This fact may reflect the intent of startup schools to remain small or it may reflect capacity limits stemming from the challenge of securing large facilities. Startups tend to draw students from a broader area than conversion schools, have longer school days, and have teachers who are less likely to be subject to the district's collective bargaining agreement.

Appendix Table D.1 shows correlations between charter school characteristics. We note that in many cases the correlations are quite high, often on the order of 0.3 to 0.5 or higher in absolute magnitude.

The Effect of Attending a Charter School on Gains in Student Achievement

This section summarizes our statistical analysis of the effect of charter schools on student gains in math and reading. As mentioned in the introduction to the chapter, we cannot use a lottery-based method of analysis as we do for the other school choice programs in San Diego, because the district does not centrally collect data on admissions lotteries. Our substitute methodology uses student fixed effects, controlling for any unobserved characteristic of students that does not change over the course of our data collection. So, for example, to the extent that charter school students differ in ability and motivation, and to the extent that these are fixed characteristics of each student, we completely remove any of these interstudent differences that do not change over time. Put differently, we estimate the average effect of a charter school on student achievement by comparing individual student's test-score trajectories during periods in which they attend and do not attend charter schools. This approach is generally much more useful than simple comparisons across students, which risk confounding the effect of charter schools with the effect of unobserved characteristics of students who are attracted to charter schools.

One word of caution is in order here. The previous section showed that charter schools share many common goals but also differ in important ways. That immediately begs the question: What does it mean to estimate the "average" effect of charter schools on student achievement? Although it seems clear that charter schools are indeed quite heterogeneous, from a policy perspective, we think that it is crucial to start with an analysis of the average effect of these schools. Indeed, this question has dominated the politics surrounding charter schools. At the same time, we would indeed like to go beyond this question to identify the types of charters that have been the most successful, at least in terms of boosting math and reading achievement. In this chapter, we make some efforts in that direction by distinguishing between startup and conversion charter schools. In theory, we could go beyond that and ask which of the school characteristics captured in our survey appear to have the greatest effect on achievement gains. We do not take this latter route because, as the previous section showed, many of the survey variables are quite highly correlated with each other, so that it is unlikely that we could obtain reliable results. The issue here is simply a lack of variation in the data. In the future, as more student data accumulate, new charters open, and, perhaps, as some charters alter their academic focus in ways that we can identify through surveys, we may be able to answer this more subtle question.

Just as there may be no such thing as the completely "typical" charter school, there may be no such thing as a "typical" charter school student. Which types of students gain the most and least from the experience offered by San Diego's charter schools? Again, because we rely on the subsample of students who switch back and forth between charters and regular public schools, our sample size requires caution. However, after presenting our "average" results, we summarize some tentative conclusions about differential effects of charters by student race.

Our initial analyses simply model either test-score gains or levels of test scores as a function of fixed effects, as well as controls for grade level and year. We used two main specifications. The first of these models gains in scaled scores on the Stanford 9 test of math and reading achievement. The second models the level of a student's test score as a function of the previous year's test scores and the same set of additional regressors.[7] We report results for both methods and typically the results are similar.

Figure 5.2 shows our calculated effect sizes from the first models (that is, the predicted effect measured as the percentage of a standard deviation of test scores in that grade span) of switching to a charter school in cases where there is a statistically significant effect. No bars, such as for high schools, indicate no statistically significant differences between charters and regular public schools for that subject in that grade span.

We find that switching to a charter school results in higher middle school math test-score gains but lower elementary math and middle

---

[7]Because adding a student fixed effect to a model with a lagged dependent variable (namely, lagged test scores) can lead to bias and inconsistency, we use the method of Anderson and Hsiao (1982) to estimate these latter models.

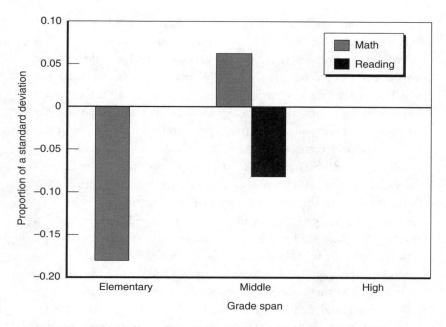

Figure 5.2—Effect of Attending a Charter School on Stanford 9 Test-Score Gains

school reading gains. The sizes of these effects are moderate, on the order of 6 to 18 percent of a standard deviation in score for that grade span and year. The estimates underlying these calculations are presented in Appendix Table D.2, along with regression estimates from the second model focusing on levels of test scores.

This same appendix table also reports the number of students included in each regression and the number of these who attend a charter. In our main specification depicted in Figure 5.2, the number of students entering our regressions ranges from about 47,000 students in the high school model to about 62,000 students in the elementary school model. Of these samples, the number of students who ever attended a charter school ranged from about 1,500 for the elementary school models up to about 5,800 for the middle school models. This suggests that although we have reasonably large numbers of charter school students, the elementary school sample will be the one least likely to reveal small (positive or negative) effects of charter schools on achievement, because of the relatively small sample size.

For a second reason we need to be cautious about sample size. To contribute to our estimate of the effect of attending a charter school, a student must attend a charter for at least one year and a regular public school for at least one year within a grade span, so that we can compare his or her test-score gains in the two types of schools. Most of our charter enrollees attend charter schools and stay in charter schools throughout the grade span. This was most prevalent in our middle school sample, where 90 percent of charter attendees are in charter schools throughout the sample period. In the elementary and high school samples, the percentages are 85 percent and 73 percent, respectively. These students did not contribute to our estimated effect of attending a charter school. This may be of special concern at the elementary school level, since there are fewer charter students overall at that level than at the middle and high school levels. Note also that the fixed-effect method should give a quite reliable estimate of the effect of attending a charter for switchers, but we cannot say for certain whether the same effect applies to students who, for instance, enroll in a charter in kindergarten and stay in charter schools throughout the sample period.

The most important implication for interpretation of our results is that when we find a zero effect of attending a charter school, we are more confident that the effect is truly zero in the middle and high school samples than in the smaller elementary school samples.

In Figure 5.3, we separately present effect sizes of switching to startup and conversion charter schools to explore whether there are performance differences between the types of schools. The figure reveals that at the elementary school level, both startups and conversions seem to produce lower test-score gains in math relative to regular public schools, but they produce identical gains in reading. At the middle school level, we can see that the conversion schools drive the overall result that charter schools are better at teaching math and worse at teaching reading.[8] Middle school startups appear to perform the same as regular middle

[8]Two large conversion schools dominate the middle school charter school sample.

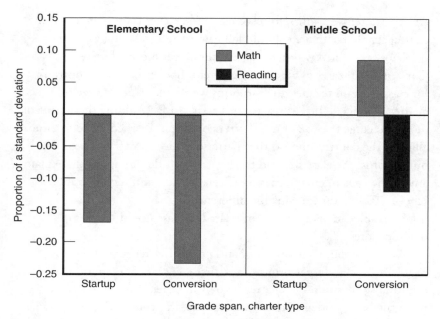

NOTE: There are no conversions at the high school level.

Figure 5.3—Effect of Attending a Startup or Conversion Charter School
on Stanford 9 Test-Score Gains

schools in both subjects. We do not break down high school results by
charter type, because all of the charter high schools in San Diego are
startup schools. (Estimates underlying these calculations can be found in
Appendix Table D.3.)

Given that we did find a few cases in which charter schools appeared
to differ significantly from regular public schools in terms of gains in
reading or math, it is natural to ask whether we can explain these
differences in terms of observable characteristics of the classrooms.
Accordingly, for the subsamples for which we had class size and detailed
teacher qualifications (credential status, highest degree earned, and years
of teaching experience), we reran our basic models and obtained very
similar results on these subsamples. Next we reestimated these models
after adding class size and controls for teacher qualifications. The idea
here is that if the simpler model showed that charter schools were more

effective, after we control for class size and teacher traits, the size of the charter school coefficient should fall toward zero, because we have (perhaps) explained why the charter school was more effective. Conversely, in cases of a negative charter school effect, after controlling for class size and teacher qualifications we should expect to see the charter school coefficient rise toward zero. In fact, adding these controls did not change the size of the charter coefficient markedly and in almost all cases the controls moved the charter dummy away from zero. In other words, the class size and teacher controls do not appear to explain any of the gaps in effectiveness between charters and regular public schools. Whatever explains the differences, it has to do with unobservable factors that are not related to class size or teacher qualifications.

We next examined whether San Diego's charter schools face startup problems and underperform in their first few years of operation, as is found in some studies of charter schools in other areas. To do this, we reran the basic student fixed-effect analysis, this time adding additional control variables indicating whether a school is in its first, second, or third year of operation.[9] Conversion schools are observed only four years or later after their conversion, so we are not able to test if conversions have difficulties in their first three years. Thus, our tests for startup problems quite literally apply only to charter schools that have started from scratch.

Our central finding changes the tenor of our earlier results on the relative performance of startups and regular public schools. Recall that as shown in Figure 5.3, startup schools performed the same as regular public schools except that they underperformed in math at the elementary school level. As shown in Table 5.6, by year four and later, startup charters show gains in reading and math that are statistically indistinguishable from gains in regular public schools. This applies to all three grade spans. Conversely, we find that elementary school startups in their initial years produce much lower test-score gains than do regular

---

[9]We also ran several alternative specifications where indicators were included for first, first two, or first three years of operation, as well as a specification assuming a linear effect of additional years of operation. These yielded qualitatively similar results. The estimates in Table 5.6 derive from the estimates in Appendix Table D.4.

Table 5.6

Estimated Effect of Attending a New Startup Charter School Measured in Proportion of Stanford 9 Test-Score Standard Deviation Units

			Measure
Elementary school	Math	1st year of startup	−0.55
		2nd year of startup	—
		3rd year of startup	−0.29
		4th year or later	—
	Reading	1st year of startup	−0.20
		2nd year of startup	—
		3rd year of startup	—
		4th year or later	—
Middle school	Math	1st year of startup	—
		2nd year of startup	0.19
		3rd year of startup	0.21
		4th year or later	—
	Reading	1st year of startup	—
		2nd year of startup	—
		3rd year of startup	—
		4th year or later	—

NOTES: Effects are calculated with student fixed effects, ordinary least squares specification, with conversion control. Blank entries indicate no statistically significant effects at the 5 percent level. There are no significant effects at the high school level.

public schools in both reading and math. Table 5.6 shows that the largest effects are found in math scores, where attending an elementary charter school in its first year of operation results in a test-score gain that is more than half a standard deviation below the average test-score gain at a noncharter school. We do not find significant year-in-operation effects for middle or high schools except in the case of middle school math, where it appears that schools in their second and third years of operation actually do *better* than those in their fourth or later year of operation.

The overall conclusion seems to be that startup charter schools in the elementary school grade span have often experienced quite serious teething pains in their first one to three years of operation, but after this point they perform at the same level as their regular school counterparts.

Startup charters at the middle and high school levels seem to perform at least at the same level as regular public schools in all years of operation.

In contrast, the results we presented in Figure 5.3 for conversion charters apply to schools that had converted from regular to charter schools more than three years earlier, so in two cases (elementary school math and middle school reading), they underperform and in middle school math they outperform the regular public schools well into their histories.

Previous researchers have noted that students often appear to need time to fully adjust to a new school environment, having lower test-score gains in their first year at a new school. For example, Solmon, Paark, and Garcia (2001) find in Arizona that the first year a student attends a charter school his or her scores may drop but subsequently recover. We try to test whether these effects are apparent in our data and, if so, whether they are more or less pronounced at charter schools than at traditional schools. Appendix Table D.5 summarizes the results of these analyses, which show that students switching to new schools do tend to have lower test-score gains. (The comparison group here is students who have been in the given type of school for four years.) Students switching to either charter or noncharter schools appear to face difficulties in their first year at a new school in elementary school math and middle school reading. At the elementary school level, the negative effect of switching schools appears only in the student's first year at a school. Middle school math scores appear to be significantly lower in the first or second year that a student enters a regular public school after having attended a charter school. Problems with changing high schools seem to appear only in the second year at a new regular public school.

As shown above, several schools target at-risk or disadvantaged students, and several more offer special programs tailored to their students. Given this ability to tailor curricula for their student populations, it is natural to ask whether some students benefit disproportionately from attending charter schools. To answer this question, we investigate differential effects by student race by rerunning our basic specifications separately for each major racial subgroup. We can then see whether the estimated effects of charter schools differ by race. (Appendix Table D.6 shows these charter school effects by race and ethnicity.)

Almost all the significant differences between charter and regular public schools arise in math. The largest of these effects are in elementary school math, where it appears that Hispanic students have smaller test-score gains, by more than one-third of a standard deviation, when switching to charter schools. This result is driven by the startup schools, in which Hispanic students have math test-score gains half a standard deviation smaller than when they do not switch to startup schools. Asian students in conversion charter schools also appear to have much lower math test-score gains. These results may drive the overall finding that elementary charter schools are not doing well in math.

At the middle school level, the results are not as clear. Hispanic middle school students have somewhat larger math test-score gains when they switch to charter schools, whereas Asian students have lower math gains. The larger math gains for Hispanics are driven by the conversion schools; in startup schools, they actually do slightly worse. Black middle school students have larger math gains only when they switch to startup schools. All of these effects are moderate in size.

At the high school level, the only difference for a specific race was for whites, who fared slightly worse in math in charter than in regular public schools.

The only significant overall charter reading effects apply to Hispanic students. Hispanic students appear to have slightly smaller reading gains when they switch to charter schools, particularly when switching to conversion charter schools. Although there is no overall charter effect for reading for middle school black students, these students do appear to do slightly better in startup schools. Startup charter schools appear to benefit middle school black students in both reading and math.

Gains Measured by the California Standards Test

Finally, we examine performance according to an alternative achievement measure. All of the previous analyses focused on student performance as measured by the norm-referenced standardized Stanford 9 test, which California used as a state test from spring 1998 through spring 2002. However, we also have available a criterion-referenced test, designed to measure whether schools are meeting content standards developed by the California Department of Education, known as the California Standards Test. We have CST data from spring 2002 through spring 2004. Because the test is not vertically scaled and therefore scores between years are not easily used to construct measures of student achievement gains, we normalize the test scores so that in each grade and in each year the average score is 0 and the standard deviation is 1. Changes between years in these measures therefore capture students' change in *relative* standing.

The results in this section differ qualitatively somewhat from the results using Stanford 9 test scores. In part this might reflect a different time period (Stanford 9 data are available from 1998 through 2002). Also, in part it might reflect the fact that with a smaller number of years of CST availability, we lack enough observations to detect meaningful effects of charter schools. In the middle and high school grade spans, we have significantly fewer charter-school-student observations in the CST models than we do in the Stanford 9 models.

With these qualifications in mind, we see in Appendix Table D.7 that according to the criterion-based measure, charter school students appear to perform better than those in traditional public schools in math at the elementary school level. This is contrary to the Stanford 9 results in which elementary charter schools underperform in math and could result because the CST data, which were gathered later in time, reflect the improvements we have already documented with startups as they gain experience. As can be seen in Appendix Table D.8, the positive math result is driven by startup schools.

Charter schools underperform in both middle school math and middle school reading. Whereas the negative reading result echoes that of the Stanford 9, the math underperformance is contrary to the Stanford 9 results, which demonstrate a positive effect of charter schools. As can be seen in Appendix Table D.8, the negative overall middle school math effect is due to the large negative effects in the startup schools. Conversion middle schools actually generate math test-score gains that are indistinguishable from those in traditional public schools. Both startup and conversion charter schools appear to face challenges in teaching middle school reading. The coefficients can be read directly as changes in proportions of a standard deviation, and they do not appear to be very large. The exception is the case of startups for middle school math, where charter schools produce slightly more than one-quarter of a standard deviation smaller gains. The negative charter school effects at the middle school level on this criterion-based test may suggest that on average charter schools may be focusing somewhat less on state-developed content standards than regular public schools do.

Conclusion

San Diego's charter schools primarily enroll students who come from areas outside the local attendance area of the nearest regular public school. This pattern probably reflects both the unique curricular focus of many of the charter schools, which would be expected to draw students from a wide area, and also that half the schools we surveyed reported targeting disadvantaged students.

Our finding that half of the charter schools report that 30 percent or less of their students come from the local attendance area also has important implications for research on the effect of charter schools on student performance. One way to gauge the effect of charter schools is to compare students' test scores with those at nearby regular public schools. There are many benefits to this research approach, but if the patterns in San Diego play out nationally, it may not produce reliable results because the student populations served at charter schools and nearby regular public schools are often quite different.

On the whole, charter schools in San Diego serve a student population that is much more likely to be economically disadvantaged, black, or Hispanic than in regular public schools. Charter schools in San Diego enroll slightly fewer special education students than do regular public schools.

Our survey shows that although for the most part charter schools in San Diego share many things, such as a strong academic focus, they differ quite a lot in other ways. For instance, their curricular emphases, beyond the basics of math, reading, and writing, differ substantially, as do the ways they choose to intervene to help students who lag behind.

Regarding charter schools' effect on test scores in reading and math, we find that charter schools in San Diego appear on the whole to be performing about as well as regular public schools, with some important exceptions. Startups appear to perform equally as well as regular schools in both math and reading, at all grade spans, by their fourth year of operation and later, but in some cases they underperform considerably in their first few years. Conversion charters, all of which were in their fourth or later year of operation, underperformed regular schools in two cases—elementary school math and middle school reading—and outperformed them in another case—middle school math.

At a more detailed level, students at elementary charter schools appear to have lower math and reading test-score gains than those in regular elementary schools. The math results include startups in their first three years only and conversion charters. The difference in elementary school reading gains reflects startup charters only and, again, only in their first few years of operation. Reading gains in middle school also appear to suffer when students attend charter schools but only for conversion charters. It may be the case that only in middle school math are traditional public schools faltering in ways that can currently be improved on with innovations by charter schools. High school performance of charter and regular schools is statistically indistinguishable, regardless of the year of operation.[10]

Just as there may be no such thing as a typical charter school, there may be no such thing as a typical charter school student. In this study we have taken a first step toward testing for variations in the effect of charter schools on students based on race. We found some evidence that charter and regular schools differ in their effect on gains in achievement by race and ethnicity. In math, Hispanic students at middle school charters outperformed their Hispanic counterparts at regular schools. In

---

[10]A quasi-experimental study of the Preuss School compares lottery winners and losers, just as we did for the VEEP, magnet, and Choice programs in the previous chapter (see McClure et al., 2005). This approach has been quite rare to date. Notably, the study finds fairly similar results to our own fixed-effect analysis of all charter schools in San Diego, with zero or small differences in test scores between Preuss attendees and students who had applied in the same year and grade but who lost the school's admissions lottery. In what may be a unique finding nationally, the authors report that graduates of the Preuss School are attending colleges in greater numbers than the comparison group. The sample sizes in this initial study are very small, but the report suggests that future research that extends beyond test scores toward longer-term outcomes could prove quite illuminating.

the same sense, Asian students underperformed in math at charter schools. In reading, Hispanic students underperformed at middle school charters, with no significant differences for other races and ethnicities.

However, when results are broken down further by charter school type, we see that black students in middle school startups outperform black students at regular schools in reading. Black middle school students appear to do well in startup charter schools in both reading and math.

If charter schools are not faring dramatically worse, or dramatically better, than regular public schools in terms of boosting student achievement, it is natural to ask whether one type of school is more cost-effective than the other. This chapter has not addressed the intricacies of charter school finance. Yet we note that charter schools appear to be less well funded than traditional schools. One of the main reasons for this is that charters often have to pay a portion of their building costs (often in the form of rent) from their general funds.[11] Teacher experience provides the clearest manifestation of this pattern of relative underfunding of charter schools, with the average charter school teacher having 8.9 years of teaching experience compared to 14.6 years for teachers in regular public schools. Similarly, 36.5 percent of charter school teachers hold a master's degree, compared to 57.6 percent of teachers in regular schools. Given these stark differences, it is indeed somewhat surprising that charter schools on the whole seem to boost student achievement at about the same rate as in regular public schools. We do note that any existing gaps in performance between the two types of schools could not be explained by variations in teacher qualifications or class size. This meshes with earlier results based on SDUSD data by Betts, Zau, and Rice (2003) that suggest that teacher qualifications play a limited role in explaining rates of student gain in achievement, especially in elementary schools.

It would have been much more dramatic to have found huge and consistent performance differences between charter and regular public schools, but what we have in fact discovered may be equally important: With some notable exceptions, we have found that charter schools are

---

[11]For a discussion of this point, see Betts, Goldhaber, and Rosenstock (2005).

faring about as well as regular public schools and are doing so with relatively less experienced teachers. This finding raises important questions about whether charter schools in San Diego may prove somewhat more cost-effective than regular public schools.

A natural question arises: Even if it is true today that charter schools tend to hire less experienced teachers than do regular public schools, does this represent a long-term pattern or merely teething pains?[12] Nothing in our data can answer this question decisively. However, conversations that we have had with several charter school leaders in San Diego and other California cities suggest that this pattern will persist for the foreseeable future. The reason is simple: The funding pressures that charter schools face relative to regular public schools are endemic and apparently long-term. Given that salaries constitute the main cost of running a school, charter schools will have no alternative but to economize by hiring a relatively young and less experienced mix of teachers.

This study suggests promising avenues for future research. First, policymakers stand to gain a lot from a detailed comparative analysis of revenue streams and costs between charter schools and regular public schools. What are the exact mechanisms that drive charters to focus on hiring teachers who are relatively new to the profession? Is this apparent underfunding a matter of policy concern? Second, our finding that in some cases conversion and startup charter schools perform differently begs questions about other aspects of charter schools that matter for student performance. Our survey data hint at some important differences, but with only 16 snapshots of charter school operations at one point in time, this first survey cannot be relied on to explain all variations in charter school outcomes. Over time, as more charters enter the district and individual charters fine-tune their academic approaches, this might become possible. Third, we desperately need to learn more about the types of students who benefit the most from attending a charter school. Our analysis by race and ethnicity represents only a first step in this direction.

---

[12]We thank Mark Schneider for raising this point.

6. Policy Implications and New Questions

Who chooses to leave their local schools and why? How do school choice and space constraints affect integration? For students who win a chance to attend a school of choice, how does it affect their achievement in math and reading? These are the three central questions that we have addressed in this report.

The first two questions are closely related. We studied integration using application data to the VEEP, magnet, and open-enrollment Choice programs. Our finding that students' own characteristics have much to do with who applies to leave their local school has direct implications for integration. For the most part, nonwhite students appear quite keen to apply to school choice programs. In spite of a shortage of spaces in option schools that necessitates admissions through a random drawing, the choice programs in San Diego clearly do increase racial and ethnic integration between white students and other students across schools. We found some evidence that choice programs integrate students of differing parental education levels. However, integration between high- and low-scoring students appears to have fallen, solely because the open-enrollment Choice program tended to segregate students in these two groups. Similarly, both the magnet and the Choice programs clearly appeared to be lowering integration between EL and non-EL students.

Among the three programs, the open-enrollment Choice program clearly has done the least to integrate students. It is alone among the programs in not providing busing. One possible interpretation of this correspondence is that the provision of busing is an important mechanism to level the school choice playing field. A second important distinction between open-enrollment and the magnet and VEEP programs is that the former places no restrictions on who may attend where. The lesson here may be that school choice can either decrease or increase integration: Proactive policies, such as subsidies for busing and limits on choice, either by matching sending and receiving schools or by providing priority to applications from certain areas, may be necessary to ensure that integration increases.

Second, even in a district with unusually high participation in choice programs, such as San Diego, limitations in supply reduce the degree to which integration actually occurs. Application patterns show that nonwhite students, students whose parents have less education, and students with lower test scores strongly wish to move to nonlocal schools and that existing choice programs cannot meet this demand. This is a fairly remarkable finding given that by 2003–2004, 28 percent of district students were already in various choice programs. The implication is that much more could be done to integrate the district were more spaces available. However, it would be very difficult to predict how a large increase in openings for nonlocal students would play out, mainly because we cannot predict whether local families would themselves choose to send their children elsewhere if there were a large influx of students from outside the neighborhood.

Our second main question, and in many people's minds the most important policy question in school choice, is whether school choice alters applicants' math and reading achievement. The best summary seems to be that *in general* students who win lotteries to attend a school through one of the three choice programs, or who switch into charters, show no statistically significant difference in reading and math achievement.

There are two crucial exceptions that we believe to be most convincing and systematic in a statistical sense. First, magnet high schools seem to produce higher math achievement. Second, all of the programs, in at least some grades and subjects, provide hints that sometimes students switching into the programs suffer temporary, typically one-year, declines in achievement. This is quite consonant with the recent literature on charter schools in other states that points to similarly temporary transition costs. (Nor is this unique to schools that accept students from outside the local attendance area: We also found some evidence that students who leave charter schools experience temporary reductions in their achievement gains once back in regular public schools.)

We are left with a mystery. We see that over one-quarter of the district's students participate in choice programs, and a large number of applications are turned away for lack of space. So, how could it be that the four school choice programs are so popular when they seem to produce growth in math and reading achievement that is only roughly the same as that in regular public schools? What makes the programs so popular?

Two explanations come to mind, with quite different implications. The first, and clearly more disturbing theory, is that parents do not know much (and are too optimistic) about the academic gains that their children would enjoy should they enter a choice program. This seems quite plausible. The district's Enrollment Options Office puts together a detailed brochure, which every family receives annually. This brochure highlights characteristics of each school very effectively, but it does not contain any direct information on the elusive concept of "school quality." Although results on the state test are published in newspapers and on the web in great detail each year, and even though these results are broken down by school and race, the published test scores do not simultaneously take into account other factors outside the school that could affect student achievement, such as variations in parental education, financial resources, and student motivation. A crude but transparent way to rephrase this idea is that parents may mistakenly think that high-scoring schools with a large percentage of white students and highly educated parents are always "good" schools. In fact, the quality of teaching may not necessarily be better than at a local school with lower scores that happens to be in a less affluent neighborhood.

A second theory is that although parents may care about math and reading achievement, there are many other aspects of a school's environment that matter as well. Our findings on schools to which students apply as well as evidence in other studies show that parents care deeply about the socioeconomic status of their children's schoolmates. But we found only limited support for the idea that parents search for schools with the highest API (the state's overall measure of student achievement). Parents may view increasing the socioeconomic status of their children's school peers as an end in itself or as a way to a better future for their children. Many mechanisms seem possible. Parents may believe that schools in more affluent areas are safer, or that these schools engender certain behaviors in children that will benefit them as adults, or that both they and their children will benefit by developing new social networks.

Future research could shed light on these questions by focusing greater attention on the types of information that parents gather, the information they have on the academic quality of various programs, and their preferences. In short, even though choice programs are holding their own academically in San Diego, we need to know more about parents' attitudes and actual knowledge. In this way, we could determine whether it is the case that parents do not know the relative quality of schools, that parents do not care about the relative quality of schools, that test scores do not fully capture students' understanding of subjects, or that researchers cannot quantify what it is that parents care about. As is so often the case, the truth may encompass all four of these scenarios.

Should SDUSD expand or contract its school choice offerings? We would argue, forcefully, that our findings do not tell us enough to make that determination. On the one hand, it is easy to show that the choice programs are very popular with parents. That alone may be enough to justify their existence. But if a policymaker were particularly focused on reading and math achievement, what then? On the whole, choice programs in San Diego are associated with roughly equal gains in math and reading achievement, with some exceptions that we have noted above. So can we justify the cost of continuing choice programs?

To answer this, we first need to state carefully that although we used quite robust statistical designs, it is possible that if we repeated this analysis five years later using a separate cohort of students and a slightly different mix of school choice options, the answers could differ somewhat.

In addition, some policymakers will question whether test scores are fully reliable measures of student achievement. It is hard to argue with an academic focus on the essential skills of reading and math, and this is why we focused on them. We argue further that our use of more than one measure of reading and math achievement lessens concerns that an individual test does not reflect the subject matter being taught. But some questions obviously remain.

Third, the question of cost efficiency does not hinge solely on the issue of whether students who enter choice programs start to boost their achievement. This is especially true in the case of charter schools. Although we found a few grade spans, types of charter schools, and subject areas for which charters were associated with higher or lower achievement growth, perhaps the most important issue affecting the cost-effectiveness of charter schools has to do with their generally lower levels of spending compared to regular public schools. If, on the whole, charter schools perform about as well as regular public schools but have lower budgets, the implication is that charter schools may be more cost-effective than regular public schools. More research on this is needed.

For the open-enrollment program, Choice, the main additional cost is the private cost to families of transporting their student to a nonlocal school. So from the point of view of a policymaker, it may be moot as to whether our "equal rate of learning" result for Choice programs versus enrolling in the local school should be any cause for concern.

More difficult is the decision concerning the programs with district-paid busing, VEEP, and magnets, because large public subsidies are at issue. Certainly, the strong pattern of positive results for high school magnets in math helps to build the case for magnets in the cost-effectiveness calculation. For VEEP, the calculus is made more difficult by the lack of any systematic effect related to math and reading achievement. But here again, there could be other benefits to VEEP that are not captured by reading and math achievement. These benefits could include academic gains in other subject areas that are not regularly tested, social networking, and improved behavioral outcomes.

Although the importance of this study to children, parents, and school administrators in San Diego seems clear, it is worth reflecting upon how policymakers in Sacramento, in Washington, D.C., and in districts statewide and nationwide might use these results. What, then, are the more general implications of our results on the effects of school choice on integration and on academic achievement?

Regarding the national debate on school choice and integration, do our results suggest that expanding parental choice will lead to greater integration, as proponents claim, or greater segregation, as critics fear? The answer depends very much on the design of the school choice program in question. The program that did the least to integrate and the most to segregate was the open-enrollment program. The VEEP and magnet programs did much better at integration, and they shared two differences from the open enrollment. First, they both provided free busing, which could be a very important factor in leveling the playing field between more and less affluent families. Only the former may have easy access to private transportation. Second, both the VEEP and magnet programs limited choice geographically, in ways designed to promote integration. These two factors, busing and geographic preferences, could prove similarly important in promoting integration in other locales.

Another lesson for policymakers outside San Diego is that it would be a mistake to interpret the actual use of school choice programs as a measure of the actual demand for them by parents. Even in San Diego, where more than one-quarter of students are already choosing nonlocal public schools, the new demand for slots in the year we examined considerably outstripped supply. This excess demand, it turns out, has important implications for integration. Because some of the most oversubscribed schools were in affluent areas, the actual amount of integration produced by the choice programs was far smaller in fall 2001 than it would have been had there been slots available to all.

Turning to the analysis of test scores, what do the generally insignificant effects of choice on achievement imply for state and national policy? Lawmakers in Sacramento should be interested to know that the two state-mandated choice programs, charter schools and the open-enrollment program, are producing gains in reading and math achievement very similar to those produced in regular public schools. These programs are highly popular with families and apparently with voters. At the national level, perhaps the most relevant issue concerns the mandate in the federal NCLB law that districts must devote some fraction of their Title I dollars to providing busing to students in certain failing schools, so these students can attend "nonfailing" schools. It seems likely that the outcomes for these NCLB-busing participants will resemble what we have found for VEEP. The key national policy question then becomes: If NCLB is concerned about boosting academic achievement in math, reading, and related core subjects, what will prove to be the more cost-effective way to help students in low-performing schools—busing or improved instruction in the low-performing schools? The answer at this point is not clear. This debate could well become one of the central education policy issues nationwide by the time NCLB is up for reauthorization in 2007.

Appendix A

Data, Methods, and Results for Chapter 2

This appendix describes the data, methods, and results for the analysis presented in Chapter 2. The analysis uses students' lottery application data to run probit models investigating the effect of student and school characteristics on the probability of applying to school choice programs.

Data and Methods

Chapter 2 uses SDUSD data on school choice applications for the VEEP, magnet, and open-enrollment programs for fall 2001. Data on student and school characteristics are from the 2000–2001 school year (the period when the students were applying for schools for fall 2001). Students do not have to reapply in subsequent years to continue to attend a choice school.[1]

Test score data come from the Stanford 9 standardized test. We have taken the mean of students' scores from the math and reading components and then standardized that to have a mean of zero and a standard deviation of 1 within each grade.

For Chapter 2, students are included in the elementary school grade span if they will be entering into third, fourth, or fifth grade in fall 2001. Students who will be in grade levels below third are excluded because there are no Stanford 9 test scores available for these younger students. Students who will be entering sixth grade are also excluded from the analysis because in San Diego, sixth graders, depending on location, enroll either in elementary or in middle school. The choice set for sixth

---

[1]Technically, magnet program students do need to reapply, but these types of "continuity" applications are not counted as magnet applications for the purposes of this analysis.

graders is therefore extremely complicated and quite different from either the elementary or middle school grades. Seventh and eighth grades are included in the middle school analysis and the high school grade span includes ninth through twelfth grades.

Distance to the local or option school is measured using each student's local elementary school as a proxy for his or her residence. Usually, the student's residence is within one to two miles of his or her local elementary school.

Some students were excluded from the analysis because they live in areas where they are allowed to choose between two or more local schools, so that we were unable to assign them values for the characteristics of the local school. Overall, roughly 10 percent of the sample was excluded on these grounds, although the percentage differs between grade spans.

The sample for the VEEP analysis includes only those students who live in an attendance area (or minimal planning area) that has an active VEEP busing pattern. This includes roughly half the students in the district.

Various methods of aggregating the option school characteristics to the choice program level were tested using the high school data, including the following: (a) using the characteristics of the closest option school; (b) taking the average across the option schools in the choice set, weighting by one over the distance to the option school; and (c) taking the average, weighting by one over distance-squared (the method used for the results reported in Chapter 2). Goodness-of-fit measures were found to be extremely similar across all three methods of aggregation.[2]

For the Academic Performance Index variable included in the probits ("Option API dummy"), the actual variable used is a dummy defined to be equal to one if the weighted mean of the API for the

---

[2]Specifically, we looked at the pseudo-R-squared (McFadden R-squared), the McKelvey-Zavoina R-squared, and the Akaike Information Criterion (AIC). The results regarding the characteristics of the student were completely robust to the method of aggregation used and the results regarding the characteristics of the local school changed only very slightly. Results for the characteristics of the option schools were more sensitive to the choice of aggregation mechanism, but the results highlighted in Chapter 2 are those that appeared to be most robust.

option schools was greater than the API at the local school. (However, for the VEEP elementary school sample, none of the students had a mean option school API less than the API at the local school, so the dummy used for that sample was set equal to one if the mean option school API was more than 200 points higher than the local API.) This dummy variable measure was used because the raw data suggested a nonmonotonic tendency in the relationship between API and the probability of applying to a program. Specifically, students were more likely to apply to schools where the API was higher than that of their local school, but of those option schools where the API gap was positive, students were no more likely to apply to schools where the API gap was larger. We also ran models using the API itself, but goodness-of-fit criteria were generally better using the dummy variable approach.

All probits allow for clustering of the error terms by attendance area. (The district uses the term "minimal planning area," or MPA, for the attendance area.) The attendance area defines the choice set for the student—that is, each student in the same MPA has the same set of schools from which to choose. Using clustering of error terms in the probit models allows us to relax the assumption that students in the same MPA have error terms that are independent of one another.[3]

Results

The tables in this appendix display the results of the probit models, showing the coefficient, the standard error of the coefficient, and the marginal effect of the variable on the probability of applying (Appendix Tables A.1 through A.3). For continuous variables, the marginal effects were calculated as the change in probability of applying for a one-unit change in the explanatory variable, calculated at the mean of the explanatory variables. For the dichotomous variables, the marginal effects show the change in probability resulting from a discrete change of the explanatory variables from zero to one.

Interpreting the results for school characteristics should be done with care because of high levels of collinearity between variables, with correlation coefficients between school characteristics sometimes

---

[3]For further information on clustering, see Wooldridge (2003).

attaining magnitudes as high as 0.8 or 0.9. In particular, the Academic Performance Index is highly correlated with many of the variables concerning the demographics of the student body. For example, for the high school sample, there are fairly high correlations between API and percentage Hispanic, percentage EL, percentage of students with high parental education, and distance.

One check on the effects of collinearity on the model is to run a simpler model that excludes many of the collinear variables. Therefore, in addition to the specification presented in Appendix Tables A.1 through A.3, we also tried a simpler specification that dropped all school characteristics except distance and API. In this simpler specification, the marginal effects on the student characteristics were very similar to the marginal effects reported in Appendix Tables A.1 through A.3. However, the results for distance and API were not as robust, and we note the main differences here.

At the elementary school level, the general patterns for distance and API hold true in the simple model, although it is not always the same choice program that exhibits significant results. For the middle school grade span, the simple model indicates that students prefer schools that are nearby, whereas there were no significant results regarding option school distance in the general model. Similarly, the simple model shows some weak evidence that students prefer schools with higher API, whereas the general model had no significant results for API at the middle school grade span.

At the high school level, the simple model arrives at a negative estimated effect of local school distance on the probability of applying to VEEP, suggesting that VEEP-eligible families would actually like their children to be farther away from home rather than closer, perhaps because of some neighborhood characteristic, such as high crime. (In the general model for VEEP, local school distance dropped out of the specification as a result of collinearity.) With respect to both option school distance and local and option school API, the simple model results for the high school sample are similar to those generated by the general model; however, there are a couple of differences regarding which school choice programs have a statistically significant effect for the API.

The magnitude of the changes that are used to calculate the effect sizes shown in Figures 2.2 and 2.3 (and for GPA in Figure 2.1) is based loosely on the size of a one standard deviation change in each of the variables. For each variable, at each grade span and for each program, we calculated the standard deviation for that variable. We then chose integers that were fairly close to the magnitude of a one standard deviation change but that would allow comparisons across grade spans, choice programs, and similar variables. For example, for all variables that indicate the percentage of the student body exhibiting a certain characteristic (e.g., percentage EL or percentage black), the graphs show the effect of a standard 10 percentage point change in each of those variables.

One drawback of the analysis presented here is that we are treating residential location as given. In reality, many families choose schools by choosing where to live. This is likely to be less true for poor and nonwhite families, who may not have as much flexibility because of a lack of available funds or discrimination in the housing market. We know of no empirical research that simultaneously estimates how families make decisions about where to live and whether and how to make use of school choice programs.

Another shortcoming of the current analysis is that the probit structure implicitly assumes that the probability of applying to one choice program is unaffected by the options offered through another choice program. Future research may be able to address this shortcoming using a multinomial logit framework.

Table A.1

Probits for Applications to the School Choice Programs: Elementary School Sample

	VEEP	Magnet	Choice
	Coefficient (Std. Err.) [Marginal Effect]	Coefficient (Std. Err.) [Marginal Effect]	Coefficient (Std. Err.) [Marginal Effect]
Entering grade 4	−0.08291 (0.05137) [−0.00294]	−0.07133 (0.05104) [−0.00222]	−0.06119 (0.04588) [−0.00357]
Entering grade 5	−0.10678 (0.08636) [−0.00375]	−0.08923* (0.04903) [−0.00276]	−0.09264** (0.04502) [−0.00534]
GPA	0.01663 (0.06329) [0.00061]	0.03139 (0.04003) [0.00100]	0.05147 (0.03573) [0.00306]
Normalized Stanford 9 score	0.11298** (0.04649) [0.00412]	−0.00686 (0.03250) [−0.00022]	0.02814 (0.02814) [0.00168]
Female	0.01769 (0.04524) [0.00064]	0.00579 (0.04467) [0.00019]	0.01814 (0.03518) [0.00108]
Black	0.12824 (0.21122) [0.00512]	0.03762 (0.07619) [0.00124]	0.14421** (0.06710) [0.00951]
Asian	0.11199 (0.16878) [0.00441]	−0.33585*** (0.09344) [−0.00863]	−0.02942 (0.05545) [−0.00172]
Hispanic	0.20819 (0.16389) [0.00741]	−0.06825 (0.07775) [−0.00214]	0.02907 (0.05195) [0.00174]
Other nonwhite race	(a)	−0.00798 (0.19868) [−0.00025]	0.17305 (0.16840) [0.01215]
English learner	0.01583 (0.05491) [0.00058]	−0.12427 (0.07994) [−0.00376]	−0.18320*** (0.06696) [−0.01017]
High parental education (more than high school)	0.00631 (0.12535) [0.00023]	0.11374** (0.05328) [0.00376]	0.01383 (0.03970) [0.00083]
Currently in VEEP	−0.17842 (0.10990) [−0.00551]	0.19152 (0.12302) [0.00750]	−0.37720** (0.15293) [−0.01600]

Table A.1 (continued)

	VEEP Coefficient (Std. Err.) [Marginal Effect]	Magnet Coefficient (Std. Err.) [Marginal Effect]	Choice Coefficient (Std. Err.) [Marginal Effect]
Currently in Choice	−0.01184 (0.21595) [−0.00043]	−0.13054 (0.09655) [−0.00368]	−0.12141 (0.08539) [−0.00653]
Currently in magnet	0.05186 (0.14758) [0.00198]	0.45305*** (0.07383) [0.02264]	−0.14230* (0.07550) [−0.00752]
Local school distance (local distance is zero for all elementary school students and thus drops out)			
Local school API	0.00294 (0.00185) [0.00011]	−0.00052 (0.00073) [−0.00002]	−0.00157* (0.00086) [−0.00009]
Local school class size	0.07577*** (0.02112) [0.00276]	−0.01177 (0.01296) [−0.00038]	−0.04194* (0.02185) [−0.00250]
Local school % English learners	0.01090* (0.00572) [0.00040]	−0.00945*** (0.00303) [−0.00030]	0.00004 (0.00376) [0.00000]
Local school % black	−0.00922 (0.01211) [−0.00034]	0.01426*** (0.00367) [0.00046]	0.00677 (0.00516) [0.00040]
Local school % Asian	−0.01111 (0.01187) [−0.00040]	0.01739*** (0.00298) [0.00056]	0.00517 (0.00390) [0.00031]
Local school % Hispanic	−0.01005 (0.01358) [−0.00037]	0.01508*** (0.00336) [0.00048]	0.00724* (0.00439) [0.00043]
Local school % high parental education	0.10425 (0.64563) [0.00380]	0.14248 (0.22596) [0.00456]	−0.20653 (0.25716) [−0.01229]
Local school % teachers with full credentials	−0.01813** (0.00746) [−0.00066]	0.00128 (0.00538) [0.00004]	0.01335* (0.00784) [0.00079]
Mean option school distance (unweighted)	−0.01046 (0.02447) [−0.00038]	−0.06037*** (0.01756) [−0.00193]	−0.07774** (0.03293) [−0.00463]

Table A.1 (continued)

	VEEP	Magnet	Choice
	Coefficient (Std. Err.) [Marginal Effect]	Coefficient (Std. Err.) [Marginal Effect]	Coefficient (Std. Err.) [Marginal Effect]
Mean option school API (weighted by 1/distance–squared) > local school API (Yes = 1)[b]	0.42637* (0.22970) [0.01455]	0.08759 (0.08166) [0.00285]	-0.27182*** (0.08905) [-0.01617]
Mean option school class size (weighted by 1/distance-squared)	-0.18741* (0.10528) [-0.00683]	0.17164 (0.13340) [0.00549]	-0.21863*** (0.07388) [-0.01301]
Mean option school % English learners (weighted by 1/distance-squared)	0.02752* (0.01670) [0.00100]	-0.01174 (0.00896) [-0.00038]	-0.02971*** (0.01053) [-0.00177]
Mean option school % black (weighted by 1/distance-squared)	0.02495 (0.02663) [0.00091]	-0.01012 (0.01038) [-0.00032]	-0.04005*** (0.01319) [-0.00238]
Mean option school % Asian (weighted by 1/distance-squared)	-0.02092 (0.01510) [-0.00076]	-0.01211 (0.01163) [-0.00039]	0.00099 (0.00906) [0.00006]
Mean option school % Hispanic (weighted by 1/distance-squared)	0.00140 (0.01283) [0.00005]	0.01368 (0.01786) [0.00044]	0.00756 (0.01189) [0.00045]
Mean option school % high parental education (weighted by 1/distance-squared)	-0.48550 (0.85923) [-0.01770]	-0.09868 (1.09120) [-0.00315]	-0.25082 (1.02455) [-0.01493]
Mean option school % teachers with full credentials (weighted by 1/distance-squared)	-0.00676 (0.04018) [-0.00025]	-0.01049 (0.00989) [-0.00034]	0.00860 (0.02183) [0.00051]
Constant	0.77842 (4.68699)	-4.78531 (3.23610)	4.61884* (2.72023)
Observations	14,339	23,800	23,963
Log likelihood	-1,311	-1,850	-3,120
LR Chi-squared	238	240	329
Pseudo R-squared	0.0833	0.0608	0.0500

Table A.1 (continued)

	VEEP	Magnet	Choice
	Coefficient (Std. Err.) [Marginal Effect]	Coefficient (Std. Err.) [Marginal Effect]	Coefficient (Std. Err.) [Marginal Effect]
McKelvey-Zavoina R-squared	0.1221	0.0915	0.0779
AIC	0.1871	0.1581	0.2631

NOTES: The option school characteristic variables are calculated by taking the mean of the characteristic across all the option schools available to that student, weighted by the inverse of the square of the distance to the option school. Standard errors are robust and allow for clustering by attendance area.

aDropped out because of collinearity.

bFor the VEEP sample, this dummy variable is set equal to one if the aggregated option school API is more than 200 points above the local school API. This change was made because, for the VEEP sample, the aggregated option school API is always greater than the local school API, so there was no variation in the dummy variable using the original measure.

*Significant at the 10 percent level.

**Significant at the 5 percent level.

***Significant at the 1 percent level.

Table A.2

Probits for Applications to the School Choice Programs: Middle School Sample

	VEEP	Magnet	Choice
	Coefficient (Std. Err.) [Marginal Effect]	Coefficient (Std. Err.) [Marginal Effect]	Coefficient (Std. Err.) [Marginal Effect]
Entering grade 8	−0.67395*** (0.07228) [−0.05704]	−0.53517*** (0.08335) [−0.02722]	−0.34595*** (0.05170) [−0.01807]
GPA	0.01879 (0.03732) [0.00155]	−0.16838*** (0.03936) [−0.00836]	−0.07934** (0.03504) [−0.00411]
Normalized Stanford 9 score	0.04998 (0.03957) [0.00413]	0.18589*** (0.03928) [0.00922]	0.12580*** (0.02716) [0.00652]
Female	0.01837 (0.03678) [0.00152]	0.06937* (0.03894) [0.00345]	−0.00020 (0.03677) [−0.00001]
Black	0.12524 (0.09819) [0.01102]	0.16044** (0.06337) [0.00890]	0.25794*** (0.07747) [0.01599]
Asian	−0.16633 (0.11498) [−0.01256]	−0.15009** (0.07378) [−0.00678]	0.02690 (0.07559) [0.00142]
Hispanic	0.16643** (0.08359) [0.01375]	−0.13496* (0.07008) [−0.00646]	−0.02900 (0.06714) [−0.00149]
Other nonwhite race	−0.17368 (0.41625) [−0.01232]	0.27131 (0.19827) [0.01767]	−0.04921 (0.22868) [−0.00243]
English learner	0.11883** (0.05412) [0.01015]	−0.08739 (0.05326) [−0.00413]	−0.01470 (0.07091) [−0.00076]
High parental education (more than high school)	0.04141 (0.05830) [0.00350]	0.11732*** (0.04090) [0.00599]	0.09303* (0.05538) [0.00493]
Currently in VEEP	−0.74277*** (0.16745) [−0.03966]	−0.51137*** (0.11286) [−0.01675]	−0.30657*** (0.11533) [−0.01235]

	VEEP	Magnet	Choice
	Coefficient (Std. Err.) [Marginal Effect]	Coefficient (Std. Err.) [Marginal Effect]	Coefficient (Std. Err.) [Marginal Effect]
Currently in Choice	−0.15983 (0.10788) [−0.01165]	−0.03767 (0.09153) [−0.00181]	0.02514 (0.10886) [0.00133]
Currently in magnet	−0.10251 (0.12137) [−0.00784]	0.23221** (0.10369) [0.01427]	0.07549 (0.09250) [0.00419]
Local school distance	0.71892*** (0.20684) [0.05947]	0.19022*** (0.07151) [0.00944]	0.00438 (0.04355) [0.00023]
Local school API	0.00123 (0.00327) [0.00010]	−0.00244 (0.00230) [−0.00012]	−0.00123 (0.00126) [−0.00006]
Local school class size	−0.08934** (0.04130) [−0.00739]	−0.00650 (0.01381) [−0.00032]	−0.08533*** (0.01384) [−0.00443]
Local school % English learners	−0.00143 (0.00851) [−0.00012]	0.01204 (0.00795) [0.00060]	−0.02611*** (0.00848) [−0.00135]
Local school % black	0.05838*** (0.01901) [0.00483]	0.01944* (0.01112) [0.00096]	0.01277 (0.00976) [0.00066]
Local school % Asian	0.00196 (0.01325) [0.00016]	0.00413 (0.00599) [0.00020]	0.00927** (0.00372) [0.00048]
Local school % Hispanic	0.03554** (0.01697) [0.00294]	0.00519 (0.00899) [0.00026]	0.03234*** (0.00880) [0.00168]
Local school % high parental education	0.00764 (0.00925) [0.00063]	0.01284 (0.00829) [0.00064]	0.00346 (0.00717) [0.00018]
Local school % teachers with full credentials	0.01808 (0.02000) [0.00150]	0.00079 (0.01389) [0.00004]	0.04670*** (0.01586) [0.00242]
Mean option school distance (unweighted)	0.06097 (0.04427) [−0.00504]	−0.02685 (0.02900) [−0.00133]	−0.03474 (0.02713) [−0.00180]
Mean option school API (weighted by 1/distance-squared) > local school API (yes = 1)	−0.19229 (0.38623) [−0.01875]	−0.14052 (0.12186) [−0.00710]	0.00152 (0.13077) [0.00008]

	VEEP	Magnet	Choice
	Coefficient (Std. Err.) [Marginal Effect]	Coefficient (Std. Err.) [Marginal Effect]	Coefficient (Std. Err.) [Marginal Effect]
Mean option school class size (weighted by 1/distance-squared)	0.02399 (0.05004) [0.00198]	0.10811* (0.05960) [0.00536]	0.01035 (0.05990) [0.00054]
Mean option school % English learners (weighted by 1/distance-squared)	0.01908 (0.04821) [0.00158]	0.12164*** (0.04171) [0.00604]	−0.08563*** (0.03047) [−0.00444]
Mean option school % black (weighted by 1/distance-squared)	−0.06162 (0.04397) [−0.00510]	0.03532** (0.01652) [0.00175]	−0.04239** (0.01659) [−0.00220]
Mean option school % Asian (weighted by 1/distance-squared)	0.03284 (0.03326) [−0.00272]	−0.03557** (0.01451) [−0.00176]	0.05250*** (0.02022) [0.00272]
Mean option school % Hispanic (weighted by 1/distance-squared)	−0.02465 (0.05266) [−0.00204]	−0.12404** (0.05384) [−0.00616]	0.06758* (0.03735) [0.00350]
Mean option school % high parental education (weighted by 1/distance-squared)	−0.02594 (0.04011) [−0.00215]	−0.02590 (0.03026) [−0.00129]	−0.02378 (0.01790) [−0.00123]
Mean option school % teachers with full credentials (weighted by 1/distance-squared)	−0.07222 (0.07383) [−0.00597]	0.03314** (0.01459) [0.00164]	−0.03415*** (0.01097) [−0.00177]
Constant	4.57209 (11.65182)	−3.63325 (3.88490)	−0.52040 (3.40988)
Observations	10,392	18,036	18,036
Log likelihood	−2,119	−2,495	−2,244
LR Chi-squared	891	1,110	524
Pseudo R-squared	0.1737	0.1819	0.1045
McKelvey-Zavoina R-squared	0.2913	0.2506	0.1389
AIC	0.4139	0.2802	0.2524

NOTES: The option school characteristic variables are calculated by taking the mean of the characteristic across all the option schools available to that student, weighted by the inverse of the square of the distance to the option school. Standard errors are robust and allow for clustering by attendance area.

*Significant at the 10 percent level.

**Significant at the 5 percent level.

***Significant at the 1 percent level.

Table A.3

Probits for Applications to the School Choice Programs:
High School Sample

	VEEP	Magnet	Choice
	Coefficient (Std. Err.) [Marginal Effect]	Coefficient (Std. Err.) [Marginal Effect]	Coefficient (Std. Err.) [Marginal Effect]
Entering grade 10	−0.40158*** (0.09705) [−0.01353]	−0.49710*** (0.09429) [−0.01577]	−0.54710*** (0.05194) [−0.02381]
Entering grade 11	−1.10396*** (0.12646) [−0.02770]	−0.80200*** (0.10795) [−0.02193]	−0.67449*** (0.04135) [−0.02691]
Entering grade 12	−1.50474*** (0.17075) [−0.03345]	−1.23187*** (0.11233) [−0.02884]	−0.76853*** (0.06113) [−0.02879]
GPA	0.08203** (0.03702) [0.00325]	0.08871*** (0.02802) [0.00345]	0.08189*** (0.02186) [0.00440]
Normalized Stanford 9 score	−0.02767 (0.03241) [−0.00110]	0.00268 (0.02549) [0.00010]	0.01660 (0.02187) [0.00089]
Female	0.10814** (0.05013) [0.00430]	0.09160*** (0.03472) [0.00358]	0.05118* (0.02647) [0.00275]
Black	0.52421*** (0.10682) [0.03017]	0.25884*** (0.06555) [0.01242]	0.25376*** (0.05860) [0.01646]
Asian	0.47564*** (0.13625) [0.02519]	−0.04035 (0.07775) [−0.00153]	−0.03941 (0.06211) [−0.00207]
Hispanic	0.51840*** (0.12861) [0.02180]	0.10018* (0.05489) [0.00406]	0.03766 (0.05614) [0.00205]
Other nonwhite race	0.45156 (0.33457) [0.02887]	0.23180 (0.18650) [0.01154]	0.40149** (0.16426) [0.03185]
English learner	−0.14052** (0.06283) [−0.00527]	−0.16375*** (0.04472) [−0.00571]	−0.05790 (0.04822) [−0.00300]

Table A.3 (continued)

	VEEP	Magnet	Choice
	Coefficient (Std. Err.) [Marginal Effect]	Coefficient (Std. Err.) [Marginal Effect]	Coefficient (Std. Err.) [Marginal Effect]
High parental education (more than high school)	0.02377 (0.05081) [0.00095]	0.07487* (0.04068) [0.00295]	0.07188** (0.02930) [0.00390]
Currently in VEEP	−0.31634*** (0.07764) [−0.00998]	−0.30212*** (0.07659) [−0.00900]	−0.14952* (0.08386) [−0.00708]
Currently in Choice	0.04385 (0.12521) [0.00181]	0.03707 (0.05707) [0.00149]	−0.01426 (0.07896) [−0.00076]
Currently in magnet	−0.15021 (0.14422) [−0.00526]	0.25259*** (0.07248) [0.01246]	−0.04009 (0.08246) [−0.00208]
Local school distance	(a)	0.03825 (0.08221) [0.00149]	−0.00728 (0.04778) [−0.00039]
Local school API	−0.01461*** (0.00360) [−0.00058]	−0.00488** (0.00232) [−0.00019]	−0.00635*** (0.00161) [−0.00034]
Local school class size	−0.18864*** (0.06396) [−0.00748]	−0.00621 (0.01524) [−0.00024]	−0.01450 (0.01804) [−0.00078]
Local school % English learners	−0.08831*** (0.02247) [−0.00350]	−0.01875* (0.01004) [−0.00073]	−0.03820*** (0.01068) [−0.00205]
Local school % black	−0.00596 (0.01643) [−0.00024]	0.00672 (0.01188) [0.00026]	−0.04087*** (0.00709) [−0.00219]
Local school % Asian	0.07481*** (0.02577) [0.00297]	0.00247 (0.00463) [0.00010]	0.01078** (0.00498) [0.00058]
Local school % Hispanic	0.04693** (0.02312) [0.00186]	−0.00732 (0.00957) [−0.00028]	−0.02309*** (0.00770) [−0.00124]
Local school % high parental education	−0.04496*** (0.01242) [−0.00178]	−0.01097* (0.00570) [−0.00043]	−0.01770*** (0.00648) [−0.00095]
Local school % teachers with full credentials	0.02379 (0.05342) [0.00094]	−0.04761* (0.02852) [−0.00185]	−0.09594*** (0.03318) [−0.00515]

Table A.3 (continued)

	VEEP	Magnet	Choice
	Coefficient (Std. Err.) [Marginal Effect]	Coefficient (Std. Err.) [Marginal Effect]	Coefficient (Std. Err.) [Marginal Effect]
Mean option school distance (unweighted)	0.07648*** (0.02881) [0.00303]	–0.04779** (0.02130) [–0.00186]	–0.06771*** (0.02328) [–0.00363]
Mean option school API (weighted by 1/distance-squared) > local school API (yes = 1)	0.86941*** (0.22966) [0.01653]	–0.04717 (0.11792) [–0.00186]	0.47378*** (0.15448) [0.03058]
Mean option school class size (weighted by 1/distance-squared)	–0.08421 (0.06945) [–0.00334]	–0.15776 (0.12187) [–0.00614]	0.08906* (0.04668) [0.00478]
Mean option school % English learners (weighted by 1/distance-squared)	–0.00778 (0.01904) [–0.00031]	–0.01531 (0.05738) [–0.00060]	–0.07194 (0.04717) [–0.00386]
Mean option school % black (weighted by 1/distance-squared)	0.09599*** (0.03488) [0.00381]	–0.05814* (0.03051) [–0.00226]	–0.00438 (0.00920) [–0.00024]
Mean option school % Asian (weighted by 1/distance-squared)	–0.01822 (0.02367) [–0.00072]	–0.01516 (0.01633) [–0.00059]	0.00633 (0.01843) [0.00034]
Mean option school % Hispanic (weighted by 1/distance-squared)	0.03841 (0.02824) [0.00152]	–0.04396 (0.05758) [–0.00171]	0.03808* (0.02293) [0.00204]
Mean option school % high parental education (weighted by 1/distance-squared)	0.02849 (0.02037) [0.00113]	–0.02303 (0.02440) [–0.00090]	–0.06814 (0.04435) [–0.00366]
Mean option school % teachers with full credentials (weighted by 1/distance-squared)	–0.01194 (0.03726) [–0.00047]	–0.10185 (0.11640) [–0.00396]	–0.21646*** (0.07070) [–0.01162]
Constant	7.51750 (7.70253)	25.60160* (14.94680)	37.77611*** (10.19064)
Observations	15,297	29,040	29,040
Log likelihood	–1,945	–3,553	–3,882
LR Chi-squared	670	1,374	1,018

Table A.3 (continued)

	VEEP	Magnet	Choice
	Coefficient (Std. Err.) [Marginal Effect]	Coefficient (Std. Err.) [Marginal Effect]	Coefficient (Std. Err.) [Marginal Effect]
Pseudo R-squared	0.1469	0.1621	0.1159
McKelvey-Zavoina R-squared	0.2944	0.2809	0.1700
AIC	0.2586	0.2471	0.2697

NOTES: The option school characteristic variables are calculated by taking the mean of the characteristic across all the option schools available to that student, weighted by the inverse of the square of the distance to the option school. Standard errors are robust and allow for clustering by attendance area.

aDropped because of collinearity.

*Significant at the 10 percent level.

**Significant at the 5 percent level.

***Significant at the 1 percent level.

Appendix B

Detailed Results on Integration

Calculation of Exposure Indices

As a simple example, suppose we wanted to calculate, for the typical English learner student, his or her "exposure" to English-fluent students in terms of the school population. This is simply the proportion of students at his or her school who are fluent. We can calculate the exposure of EL students to fluent students as

$$\sum\left(\frac{x_i}{X}\frac{y_i}{t_i}\right)$$

where

x_i = the number of EL students at school i,
X = total number of EL students in the district,
y_i = number of English-fluent students at school i, and
t_i = total population of school i.

Thus, the exposure index above is simply a weighted average of the proportion of students who are English-fluent at each school, with schools' shares of the overall EL population serving as the weights.

Applicant, Lottery Winner, and Enrollment, Appendix Tables B.1 Through B.15

This portion of the appendix shows average percentage differences in racial and other forms of school composition between applicants' choice and local schools based on applications, lottery outcomes, and actual enrollment decisions. Appendix Tables B.4, B.8, and B.12 are the analogs to Table 3.1 in the text and show the district-level results displayed in Figures 3.2 through 3.4. The remaining tables break down, for interested readers, the district-level statistics by grade span, program type, and integrating criteria. For example, Appendix Tables B.1 through B.3 are used to create Table 3.1, Appendix Tables B.5 through B.7 are used to create the summary table, Appendix Table B.4, and so on.

Recall that to calculate the average differences experienced by students after adjusting for lottery outcomes (as in Appendix Tables B.2, B.6, B.10 and B.14), we include all students who apply to a given school choice program but set to zero the change in the school composition that they would experience in any cases where all of their applications to a given program (VEEP, magnet, or Choice) lost in the lottery process. Similarly, to calculate these average differences after adjusting based on those who actually enroll, we set to zero the change in composition experienced by all applicants who do not enroll.

Exposure Indices Calculation, Appendix Tables B.16 Through B.19

This portion of the appendix presents exposure indices for all student groups examined in this study. Appendix Tables B.16 through B.19 are the basis for Figure 3.5 in the text. Refer to the beginning of this appendix for an example of how we calculate districtwide changes in exposure.

Table B.1

Average Percentage Differences in the Racial/Ethnic Makeup at Option and Local Schools of Applicants for All Applications, by Applicant's Race, Grade Span, and Program Type

	Elementary School Analysis Student's Own Race					Middle School Analysis Student's Own Race					High School Analysis Student's Own Race				
	White	Black	Asian	Hispanic	Other	White	Black	Asian	Hispanic	Other	White	Black	Asian	Hispanic	Other
VEEP															
% white difference	42.5	48.2	39.9	45.6	51.1	34.7	37.0	39.7	32.4	37.0	37.7	39.7	39.5	37.2	25.0
% black difference	-8.3	-14.2	-5.4	-7.0	-0.7	-14.8	-17.9	-13.6	-13.1	-19.0	-14.4	-27.0	-13.2	-16.9	-8.5
% Asian/Pacific Islander difference	0.5	1.5	0.1	3.0	5.1	-7.2	-8.3	-12.9	-0.4	5.0	-17.5	-10.0	-17.6	-3.1	10.0
% Hispanic difference	-35.5	-36.2	-35.4	-42.3	-56.0	-13.6	-11.4	-13.7	-19.2	-23.0	-6.4	-2.2	-9.6	-17.1	-26.0
Number of applications	59	238	85	687	7	65	258	73	653	1	25	214	189	356	2
Magnet															
% white difference	0.7	8.2	13.2	13.9	5.0	1.7	11.0	3.8	8.8	8.2	2.5	18.4	14.7	19.2	12.1
% black difference	7.5	4.7	6.7	4.6	6.2	7.8	-0.9	0.4	-0.5	7.3	0.7	-15.5	-8.1	-10.0	-1.8
% Asian/Pacific Islander difference	-1.8	-1.3	-6.0	0.6	-6.4	-2.5	-1.8	-1.9	3.6	-7.8	-8.3	-8.6	-9.8	-9.1	-2.6
% Hispanic difference	-7.0	-12.2	-14.6	-20.0	-5.4	-7.8	-9.2	-2.5	-12.6	-9.0	3.8	5.4	2.2	-1.0	-8.3
Number of applications	441	575	135	667	15	197	438	161	353	6	259	499	224	614	24
Choice															
% white difference	9.1	6.8	9.8	7.6	4.4	11.5	14.0	12.8	17.1	12.0	14.0	13.3	17.8	15.6	13.8
% black difference	-2.4	-5.2	-1.0	-2.6	-0.2	-4.6	-5.6	-4.3	-5.8	-3.3	-3.0	-5.5	-4.5	-2.2	-6.9
% Asian/Pacific Islander difference	-0.3	0.2	-3.4	-0.7	-3.0	-0.9	-7.8	-2.8	-2.9	9.0	-4.9	-7.0	-7.3	-7.2	0.9
% Hispanic difference	-6.5	-2.1	-5.4	-4.3	-1.5	-5.8	-0.6	-5.6	-8.5	-18.0	-6.8	-0.6	-6.5	-6.4	-8.7
Number of applications	828	443	274	764	23	270	162	107	211	4	388	276	239	380	19

Table B.2

Average Percentage Differences in the Racial/Ethnic Makeup at Option and Local Schools of Applicants, Adjusted for Lottery Results, by Applicant's Race, Grade Span, and Program Type

	Elementary School Analysis — Student's Own Race					Middle School Analysis — Student's Own Race					High School Analysis — Student's Own Race				
	White	Black	Asian	Hispanic	Other	White	Black	Asian	Hispanic	Other	White	Black	Asian	Hispanic	Other
VEEP															
% white difference	12.2	10.9	12.5	13.0	N/A	17.3	10.3	10.0	15.3	N/A	13.1	12.8	25.1	15.1	21.5
% black difference	-2.4	-2.2	-0.8	-2.4	N/A	-7.8	-5.4	-2.6	-5.7	N/A	-3.0	-5.8	-7.4	-5.9	-9.0
% Asian/Pacific Islander difference	0.3	0.4	0.0	0.5	N/A	-1.2	-2.1	-0.3	0.4	N/A	-8.1	-6.6	-14.6	-3.5	2.0
% Hispanic difference	-10.2	-9.2	-11.8	-11.4	N/A	-9.0	-3.0	-7.3	-10.1	N/A	-2.4	-0.6	-3.7	-5.8	-15.0
Number of winners	9	53	21	145	0	29	50	19	288	0	7	51	101	111	1
Magnet															
% white difference	-0.9	3.9	2.0	5.5	4.3	-1.8	0.8	-0.6	0.8	-1.2	-0.2	6.8	6.3	7.4	6.8
% black difference	4.0	2.0	2.3	1.5	-1.5	5.4	-1.1	-0.3	-0.5	2.2	-1.5	-7.3	-4.3	-4.8	-2.3
% Asian/Pacific Islander difference	-1.6	0.1	-0.6	-0.3	-7.1	0.7	2.2	1.6	2.9	1.5	-3.2	-3.8	-5.6	-4.4	-4.2
% Hispanic difference	-1.9	-6.3	-3.8	-7.2	4.1	-4.5	-2.2	-0.6	-3.4	-2.7	4.3	4.0	3.0	1.3	-0.6
Number of winners	160	168	34	237	3	98	151	93	117	3	121	163	85	236	10
Choice															
% white difference	3.8	2.4	2.1	2.7	4.8	4.8	3.7	3.3	3.5	N/A	5.6	3.0	5.1	5.6	5.4
% black difference	-1.0	-1.0	-0.6	-1.4	-2.4	-4.0	-1.9	-2.2	-2.3	N/A	-2.0	-2.5	-2.0	-1.9	-4.5
% Asian/Pacific Islander difference	-0.5	-0.8	-0.6	-0.4	-0.7	-0.9	-2.1	-0.1	-1.3	N/A	-0.9	-0.7	-1.1	-1.0	0.8
% Hispanic difference	-2.3	-0.6	-1.0	-1.0	-1.8	0.1	0.3	-1.1	0.1	N/A	-3.2	0.2	-2.3	-2.8	-2.5
Number of winners	253	74	44	168	9	97	30	33	52	0	151	34	56	80	10

Table B.3

Average Percentage Differences in the Racial/Ethnic Makeup at Option and Local Schools of Applicants, Adjusted for Actual Enrollment, by Applicant's Race, Grade Span, and Program Type

	Elementary School Analysis Student's Own Race					Middle School Analysis Student's Own Race					High School Analysis Student's Own Race				
	White	Black	Asian	Hispanic	Other	White	Black	Asian	Hispanic	Other	White	Black	Asian	Hispanic	Other
VEEP															
% white difference	3.8	6.6	4.1	6.9	N/A	8.8	7.8	9.2	11.8	N/A	7.5	8.8	17	8.9	N/A
% black difference	-0.4	-1.4	-0.4	-1.1	N/A	-5.0	-4.0	-1.9	-4.5	N/A	-1.7	-3.7	-5.4	-4.1	N/A
% Asian/Pacific Islander difference	0.0	0.2	0.2	0.4	N/A	-1.8	-1.8	-0.2	0.1	N/A	-5.4	-4.9	-10.4	-2.8	N/A
% Hispanic difference	-3.5	-5.5	-4.1	-6.2	N/A	-2.2	-2.1	-7.3	-7.6	N/A	-0.5	-0.3	-1.6	-2.1	N/A
Number enrolled	3	15	7	59	0	13	32	14	190	0	4	32	67	60	0
Magnet															
% white difference	-0.5	1.7	1.5	2.1	4.3	-0.2	0.2	-0.1	0.7	4.5	0.9	4.1	3.9	4.6	6.2
% black difference	2.6	1.1	1.2	1.1	-1.5	2.6	-0.3	-0.2	-1.0	0.2	-1.4	-4.1	-2.7	-3.2	-3.5
% Asian/Pacific Islander difference	0.1	0.2	-0.4	0.1	-7.1	-0.2	1.5	0.6	2.2	-5.7	-2.3	-3.0	-3.0	-3.2	-2.4
% Hispanic difference	-2.2	-3.1	-2.4	-3.4	4.1	-2.5	-1.5	-0.3	-2.0	0.8	2.4	2.8	1.4	1.5	-0.7
Number enrolled	40	56	8	65	3	44	58	81	60	2	64	75	50	117	5
Choice															
% white difference	2.6	0.8	1.5	1.1	1.5	3.9	2.7	2.1	2.8	N/A	3.9	2.0	2.4	3.2	6.1
% black difference	-0.6	0.2	-0.6	-0.7	-1.1	-3.0	-1.3	-1.3	-1.5	N/A	-1.1	-1.7	-0.8	-1.2	-4.2
% Asian/Pacific Islander difference	0.1	0.0	-0.3	0.0	-1.2	-1.5	-1.6	-0.3	-1.1	N/A	-0.2	-0.7	-0.4	-0.7	0.9
% Hispanic difference	-2.1	-1.1	-0.7	-0.5	0.6	0.7	0.2	-0.5	-0.2	N/A	-2.9	0.5	-1.4	-1.4	-3.5
Number enrolled	147	38	36	89	7	71	23	22	28	0	105	24	33	50	9

Table B.4
Average Percentage Differences in School-Level Student Achievement at Option and Local Schools, by Applicant's Achievement and Program Type

	Applicant Analysis Student's Achievement Level			Lottery Winner Analysis Student's Achievement Level			Actual Enrollment Analysis Student's Achievement Level		
	Above Median	Below Median	All	Above Median	Below Median	All	Above Median	Below Median	All
VEEP									
% above median math difference	30.9	30.6	30.7	13.0	10.3	11.1	8.8	7.3	7.6
% above median reading difference	34.3	34.0	34.0	14.2	11.3	12.2	9.3	8.0	8.3
% above median total difference	34.2	33.8	33.9	14.1	11.3	12.1	9.4	8.0	8.3
Number of applications	833	1,575	2,408	300	467	767	172	279	451
Magnet									
% above median math difference	6.1	11.1	8.7	2.0	3.7	2.9	1.4	2.4	1.9
% above median reading difference	8.3	13.7	11.1	2.3	4.3	3.3	1.7	2.7	2.2
% above median total difference	7.5	12.8	10.2	2.2	4.0	3.1	1.6	2.7	2.2
Number of applications	1,690	1,951	3,681	706	606	1,312	377	266	643
Choice									
% above median math difference	12.6	10.3	11.6	5.3	2.9	4.2	3.9	1.9	3.0
% above median reading difference	12.6	10.7	11.8	5.0	2.7	3.9	3.6	1.7	2.8
% above median total difference	13.2	11.1	12.3	5.4	3.0	4.3	3.9	2.0	3.0
Number of applications	1,857	1,421	3,318	546	262	808	377	162	539

NOTES: The differences shown are those implied by applications, those implied by lottery results, and those based on actual enrollment. Data are aggregated to the district level.

Table B.5

Average Percentage Differences in School-Level Student Achievement at Option and Local Schools of Applicants for All Applications, by Applicant's Achievement Level, Grade Span, and Program Type

	Elementary School Analysis Student's Achievement Level			Middle School Analysis Student's Achievement Level			High School Analysis Student's Achievement Level		
	Above Median	Below Median	All	Above Median	Below Median	All	Above Median	Below Median	All
VEEP									
% above median math difference	38.1	36.8	37.2	29.2	29.7	29.6	26.5	26.7	26.5
% above median reading difference	44.0	42.2	42.7	33.0	33.1	33.1	27.2	28.4	27.9
% above median total difference	42.9	41.3	41.8	32.5	32.8	32.7	28.3	29.0	28.8
Number of applications	243	394	637	322	703	1,025	268	478	746
Magnet									
% above median math difference	7.1	10.1	8.7	3.7	9.1	6.2	7.5	12.8	10.5
% above median reading difference	9.9	13.0	11.5	6.1	12.5	9.2	9.1	14.7	12.3
% above median total difference	8.7	11.7	10.3	5.4	11.5	8.2	8.5	14.2	11.7
Number of applications	454	486	940	569	546	1,155	667	919	1,586
Choice									
% above median math difference	8.3	8.4	8.3	14.2	15.0	14.5	16.1	9.8	13.1
% above median reading difference	8.8	8.2	8.5	14.4	15.4	14.8	15.5	10.6	13.2
% above median total difference	8.8	8.6	8.7	14.9	15.9	15.3	16.9	11.1	14.1
Number of applications	730	537	1,267	461	288	749	666	596	1,302

Table B.6

Average Percentage Differences in School-Level Student Achievement at Option and Local Schools of Applicants, Adjusted for Lottery Results, by Applicant's Achievement Level, Grade Span, and Program Type

	Elementary School Analysis Student's Achievement Level			Middle School Analysis Student's Achievement Level			High School Analysis Student's Achievement Level		
	Above Median	Below Median	All	Above Median	Below Median	All	Above Median	Below Median	All
VEEP									
% above median math difference	11.6	9.2	10.0	12.8	11.5	11.9	13.7	8.7	10.6
% above median reading difference	13.5	10.5	11.5	14.9	12.8	13.4	13.8	9.0	10.8
% above median total difference	13.0	10.3	11.2	14.4	12.7	13.2	14.3	9.2	11.1
Number of winners	50	86	136	120	253	373	130	128	258
Magnet									
% above median math difference	1.8	3.3	2.6	0.3	2.4	1.3	3.5	4.7	4.2
% above median reading difference	2.1	4.0	3.2	0.9	3.2	1.9	3.7	5.0	4.4
% above median total difference	1.8	3.5	2.7	0.8	3.0	1.8	3.6	4.9	4.3
Number of winners	134	144	278	270	172	442	302	290	592
Choice									
% above median math difference	2.9	1.4	2.3	6.1	3.2	4.9	6.8	4.1	5.5
% above median reading difference	3.0	1.4	2.3	5.7	2.8	4.5	6.1	3.7	5.0
% above median total difference	3.0	1.5	2.4	6.3	3.2	5.0	6.9	4.1	5.6
Number of winners	183	96	279	150	57	207	213	109	322

Table B.7

Average Percentage Differences in School-Level Student Achievement at Option and Local Schools of Applicants, Adjusted for Actual Enrollment, by Applicant's Achievement Level, Grade Span, and Program Type

	Elementary School Analysis Student's Achievement Level			Middle School Analysis Student's Achievement Level			High School Analysis Student's Achievement Level		
	Above Median	Below Median	All	Above Median	Below Median	All	Above Median	Below Median	All
VEEP									
% above median math difference	5.7	5.0	5.2	9.3	8.7	8.8	8.9	5.3	6.6
% above median reading difference	6.8	5.4	5.9	10.6	9.7	9.9	8.7	5.3	6.6
% above median total difference	6.5	5.5	5.8	10.3	9.6	9.8	9.2	5.5	6.9
Number enrolled	17	33	50	73	168	241	82	78	160
Magnet									
% above median math difference	0.8	1.3	1.1	0.4	1.7	1.0	2.5	3.2	2.9
% above median reading difference	1.5	1.8	1.6	0.8	2.0	1.3	2.7	3.4	3.1
% above median total difference	1.2	1.5	1.4	0.7	2.0	1.3	2.7	3.4	3.1
Number enrolled	44	48	92	167	76	243	166	142	308
Choice									
% above median math difference	2.1	1.1	1.7	4.5	1.8	3.4	4.8	2.6	3.7
% above median reading difference	2.2	1.1	1.8	4.2	1.7	3.2	4.3	2.3	3.3
% above median total difference	2.2	1.2	1.8	4.6	1.9	3.5	4.8	2.6	3.7
Number enrolled	120	60	180	112	30	142	145	72	217

Table B.8

Average Percentage Differences in Parental Education Levels at Option and Local Schools of Applicants, by Applicant's Parental Education Level and Program Type

	Applicant Analysis Student's Parental Education Level			Lottery Winner Analysis Student's Parental Education Level			Actual Enrollment Analysis Student's Parental Education Level		
	High	Low	Unknown	High	Low	Unknown	High	Low	Unknown
VEEP									
% high parental education difference	24.1	30.4	31.8	10.5	11.1	10.9	7.5	6.8	7.7
% low parental education difference	-14.1	-19.6	-18.3	-5.4	-5.3	-4.7	-3.7	-3.3	-3.0
% unknown parental education difference	-10.0	-10.7	-13.4	-5.2	-5.6	-6.1	-3.8	-3.4	-4.7
Number of applications	532	717	1,663	203	209	473	131	112	253
Magnet									
% high parental education difference	5.1	11.7	9.8	0.0	3.8	4.4	0.0	2.8	2.0
% low parental education difference	-9.6	-12.2	-14.9	-2.7	-4.0	-6.4	-1.7	-1.7	-2.0
% unknown parental education difference	4.4	0.5	5.2	2.7	0.3	2.1	1.7	-1.1	0.0
Number of applications	1,324	731	2,553	529	268	882	291	129	308
Choice									
% high parental education difference	12.7	10.9	10.0	4.3	3.5	3.6	2.9	2.1	1.4
% low parental education difference	-7.6	-7.7	-5.1	-2.2	-2.1	-2.0	-1.5	-1.3	-0.9
% unknown parental education difference	-5.1	-3.3	-4.9	-2.0	-1.4	-1.6	-1.3	-0.8	-0.5
Number of applications	1,386	602	2,400	410	126	555	287	91	304

NOTES: The differences shown are those implied by applications, those implied by lottery results, and those based on actual enrollment. Data are aggregated to the district level.

Table B.9

Average Percentage Differences in Parental Education Levels at Option and Local Schools of Applicants for All Applications, by Applicant's Parental Education Level, Grade Span, and Program Type

	Elementary School Analysis Student's Parental Education Level			Middle School Analysis Student's Parental Education Level			High School Analysis Student's Parental Education Level		
	High	Low	Unknown	High	Low	Unknown	High	Low	Unknown
VEEP									
% high parental education difference	32.7	37.1	37.6	23.1	24.6	28.4	21.4	29.0	25.4
% low parental education difference	−25.8	−30.0	−26.3	−15.0	−13.4	−12.9	−8.8	−13.9	−10.9
% unknown parental education difference	−6.9	−7.1	−11.4	−8.1	−10.7	−15.1	−12.7	−15.3	−14.6
Number of applications	96	262	718	195	248	607	241	207	338
Magnet									
% high parental education difference	8.4	14.0	10.6	8.5	11.4	13.7	1.0	10.7	4.4
% low parental education difference	−18.3	−27.3	−20.4	−8.1	−10.2	−12.4	−6.1	−5.9	−5.6
% unknown parental education difference	9.9	13.3	9.9	−0.4	−1.0	−1.1	4.8	−5.0	0.9
Number of applications	312	184	1,337	410	162	583	602	385	633
Choice									
% high parental education difference	10.3	5.7	9.2	12.1	12.9	11.6	15.1	14.2	11.8
% low parental education difference	−6.1	−7.8	−4.8	−5.9	−7.7	−5.2	−9.8	−7.6	−6.1
% unknown parental education difference	−4.2	2.1	−4.4	−5.9	−5.0	−6.1	−5.5	−6.9	−6.0
Number of applications	488	220	1,624	330	109	315	568	273	461

133

Table B.10

Average Percentage Differences in Parental Education Levels at Option and Local Schools of Applicants, Adjusted for Lottery Results, by Applicant's Parental Education Level, Grade Span, and Program Type

	Elementary School Analysis Student's Parental Education Level			Middle School Analysis Student's Parental Education Level			High School Analysis Student's Parental Education Level		
	High	Low	Unknown	High	Low	Unknown	High	Low	Unknown
VEEP									
% high parental education difference	10.1	8.7	10.5	11.0	12.2	12.9	10.3	10.9	7.2
% low parental education difference	-8.3	-7.4	-7.2	-6.9	-5.2	-3.8	-3.9	-4.0	-2.6
% unknown parental education difference	-1.8	-1.3	-3.3	-4.0	-6.7	-8.8	-6.5	-7.1	-4.7
Number of winners	21	46	161	69	104	213	113	59	99
Magnet									
% high parental education difference	3.1	5.1	5.2	2.9	3.9	4.7	-3.5	3.4	2.4
% low parental education difference	-5.9	-9.5	-9.6	-2.3	-3.0	-4.0	-1.7	-2.7	-1.9
% unknown parental education difference	2.9	4.4	4.4	-0.5	-0.7	-0.5	5.1	-0.7	-0.5
Number of winners	93	50	459	193	58	211	243	160	212
Choice									
% high parental education difference	2.3	2.3	3.8	3.4	3.2	2.9	6.1	4.8	3.6
% low parental education difference	-1.7	-2.1	-2.6	-0.3	-1.3	0.0	-3.6	-2.6	-1.6
% unknown parental education difference	-0.6	-0.2	-1.2	-2.8	-1.7	-2.7	-2.6	-2.3	-2.1
Number of winners	125	47	376	99	27	86	186	52	93

Table B.11

Average Percentage Differences in Parental Education Levels at Option and Local Schools of Applicants, Adjusted for Actual Enrollment, by Applicant's Parental Education Level, Grade Span, and Program Type

	Elementary School Analysis Student's Parental Education Level			Middle School Analysis Student's Parental Education Level			High School Analysis Student's Parental Education Level		
	High	Low	Unknown	High	Low	Unknown	High	Low	Unknown
VEEP									
% high parental education difference	5.3	4.4	4.9	7.8	8.5	9.9	7.7	4.3	4.6
% low parental education difference	-5.7	-3.5	-3.4	-4.9	-4.2	-3.2	-2.8	-1.0	-1.9
% unknown parental education difference	0.4	-0.9	-1.5	-2.9	-4.1	-6.6	-5.0	-3.4	-2.8
Number enrolled	13	17	54	40	66	143	78	29	56
Magnet									
% high parental education difference	3.3	1.7	2.7	1.8	2.9	2.5	-2.3	3.0	0.5
% low parental education difference	-3.6	-2.1	-3.6	-1.6	-2.0	-1.8	-1.2	-1.5	0.0
% unknown parental education difference	0.3	0.4	0.9	-0.1	-0.7	-0.6	3.5	-1.6	-0.6
Number enrolled	37	13	122	113	37	95	141	79	91
Choice									
% high parental education difference	1.8	1.5	0.9	2.4	1.9	2.4	4.0	2.8	2.3
% low parental education difference	-1.3	-1.4	-1.1	-0.1	-0.8	-0.1	-2.5	-1.5	-1.0
% unknown parental education difference	-0.4	-0.1	0.2	-2.1	-1.0	-2.1	-1.5	-1.3	-1.3
Number enrolled	83	36	198	75	20	49	129	35	57

Table B.12

Average Percentage Differences in the Proportion of English Learners at Option and Local Schools, by Applicant's English-Learner Status and Program Type

	Applicant Analysis Student EL Status		Lottery Winner Analysis Student EL Status		Actual Enrollment Analysis Student EL Status	
	EL	Non-EL	EL	Non-EL	EL	Non-EL
VEEP						
% EL difference	−33.0	−25.2	−10.6	−8.1	−6.3	−4.9
Number of applications	1,199	1,713	362	523	196	300
Magnet						
% EL difference	−22.3	−12.6	−8.6	−4.2	−3.6	−2.2
Number of applications	900	3,708	304	1,375	115	613
Choice						
% EL difference	−8.8	−7.4	−2.5	−2.1	−0.8	−1.4
Number of applications	774	3,614	152	939	86	596

NOTES: The differences shown are those implied by applications, those implied by lottery results, and those based on actual enrollment. Data are aggregated to the district level.

Table B.13

Average Percentage Differences in the Proportion of English Learners at Option and Local Schools of Applicants for All Applications, by Applicant's English-Learner Status, Grade Span, and Program Type

	Elementary School Analysis Student EL Status		Middle School Analysis Student EL Status		High School Analysis Student EL Status	
	EL	Non-EL	EL	Non-EL	EL	Non-EL
VEEP						
% EL difference	−47.5	−40.7	−20.8	−18.7	−24.9	−16.4
Number of applications	515	561	459	591	225	561
Magnet						
% EL difference	−30.6	−17.2	−16.9	−12.3	−14.5	−7.7
Number of applications	405	1,428	191	964	304	1,316
Choice						
% EL difference	−7.9	−6.2	−12.3	−7.1	−9.0	−9.8
Number of applications	442	1,890	111	643	221	1,081

Table B.14

Average Percentage Differences in the Proportion of English Learners at Option and Local Schools of Applicants, Adjusted for Lottery Results, by Applicant's English-Learner Status, Grade Span, and Program Type

	Elementary School Analysis Student EL Status		Middle School Analysis Student EL Status		High School Analysis Student EL Status	
	EL	Non-EL	EL	Non-EL	EL	Non-EL
VEEP						
% EL difference	-13.8	-11.0	-9.0	-8.9	-9.3	-5.8
Number of winners	117	111	184	202	61	210
Magnet						
% EL difference	-11.1	-7.0	-7.0	-3.4	-6.5	-2.3
Number of winners	133	469	64	398	107	508
Choice						
% EL difference	-2.2	-2.1	-2.0	-1.2	-3.3	-2.6
Number of winners	89	459	21	191	42	289

Table B.15

Average Percentage Differences in the Proportion of English Learners at Option and Local Schools of Applicants, Adjusted for Actual Enrollment, by Applicant's English-Learner Status, Grade Span, and Program Type

	Elementary School Analysis Student EL Status		Middle School Analysis Student EL Status		High School Analysis Student EL Status	
	EL	Non-EL	EL	Non-EL	EL	Non-EL
VEEP						
% EL difference	-6.5	-5.8	-6.8	-6.4	-3.9	-3.1
Number enrolled	44	40	120	129	32	131
Magnet						
% EL difference	-4.0	-3.2	-3.0	-2.1	-3.7	-1.7
Number enrolled	37	135	28	217	50	261
Choice						
% EL difference	-0.3	-1.5	-1.2	-0.8	-1.7	-1.6
Number enrolled	48	269	12	132	26	195

Table B.16

Districtwide Exposure Indices, by Race

Exposure	White Exposure		
	To Blacks	To Asians	To Hispanics
Actual exposure index in the district	0.11364	0.16964	0.27614
Counterfactual exposure index if those who entered into option schools through any choice program had remained at their local school	0.11228	0.16835	0.27252
Net effect on exposure index of all choice programs	0.00136	0.00130	0.00362
Net effect on exposure index of all choice programs (%)	1.21430	0.77092	1.32924
Net effect of VEEP program	0.00081	0.00089	0.00299
Net effect of VEEP program (%)	0.72415	0.52920	1.09661
Net effect of magnet program	0.00061	0.00009	0.00060
Net effect of magnet program (%)	0.54080	0.05139	0.21930
Net effect of choice program	–0.00007	0.00028	–0.00001
Net effect of choice program (%)	–0.06555	0.16672	–0.00481

Exposure	Black Exposure		
	To Whites	To Asians	To Hispanics
Actual exposure index in the district	0.19598	0.18199	0.37314
Counterfactual exposure index if those who entered into option schools through any choice program had remained at their local school	0.19363	0.18342	0.37618
Net effect on exposure index of all choice programs	0.00235	–0.00143	–0.00304
Net effect on exposure index of all choice programs (%)	1.21430	–0.77716	–0.80773
Net effect of VEEP program	0.00140	–0.00078	–0.00203
Net effect of VEEP program (%)	0.72415	–0.42263	–0.53886
Net effect of magnet program	0.00105	–0.00036	–0.00053
Net effect of magnet program (%)	0.54080	–0.19831	–0.13967
Net effect of choice program	–0.00013	0.00032	–0.00055
Net effect of choice program (%)	–0.06555	–0.17260	–0.14683

Exposure	Asian Exposure		
	To Whites	To Blacks	To Hispanics
Actual exposure index in the district	0.24914	0.15498	0.27442
Counterfactual exposure index if those who entered into option schools through any choice program had remained at their local school	0.24724	0.15619	0.27529
Net effect on exposure index of all choice programs	0.00191	−0.00121	−0.00087
Net effect on exposure index of all choice programs (%)	0.77092	−0.77716	−0.31437
Net effect of VEEP program	0.00131	−0.00066	−0.00030
Net effect of VEEP program (%)	0.52920	−0.42263	−0.10734
Net effect of magnet program	0.00013	−0.00031	−0.00035
Net effect of magnet program (%)	0.05139	−0.19831	−0.12678
Net effect of choice program	0.00041	−0.00027	−0.00028
Net effect of choice program (%)	0.16672	−0.17260	−0.10040

Exposure	Hispanic Exposure		
	To Whites	To Blacks	To Asians
Actual exposure index in the district	0.19432	0.15226	0.13149
Counterfactual exposure index if those who entered into option schools through any choice program had remained at their local school	0.19177	0.15350	0.13191
Net effect on exposure index of all choice programs	0.00255	−0.00124	−0.00041
Net effect on exposure index of all choice programs (%)	1.32924	−0.80773	−0.31437
Net effect of VEEP program	0.00210	−0.00083	−0.00014
Net effect of VEEP program (%)	1.09661	−0.53886	−0.10734
Net effect of magnet program	0.00042	−0.00021	−0.00017
Net effect of magnet program (%)	0.21930	−0.13967	−0.12678
Net effect of choice program	−0.00001	−0.00023	−0.00013
Net effect of choice program (%)	−0.00481	−0.14682	−0.10040

Table B.17

Districtwide Exposure Indices, by Student Achievement, Based on the Average of Math and Reading Performance

Exposure	Below-Median Performers to Above-Median Performers
Actual exposure index in the district	0.41656
Counterfactual exposure index if those who entered into option schools through any choice program had remained at their local school	0.41758
Net effect on exposure index of all choice programs	−0.00102
Net effect on exposure index of all choice programs (%)	−0.24427
Net effect of VEEP	0.00062
Net effect of VEEP (%)	0.14848
Net effect of magnet	0.00035
Net effect of magnet (%)	0.08382
Net effect of Choice	−0.00195
Net effect of Choice (%)	−0.46673

NOTE: Because above- and below-median performers are represented equally in the district (by construction), the exposure of below-median performers to above-median performers equals the exposure of above-median performers to below-median performers.

Table B.18

Districtwide Exposure Indices, by Parental Education Levels

Exposure	High Parental Education		Low Parental Education		Unknown Parental Education	
	To Low Parental Education	To Unknown Parental Education	To High Parental Education	To Unknown Parental Education	To High Parental Education	To Low Parental Education
Actual exposure indices in the district	0.23631	0.21599	0.34645	0.24021	0.34410	0.26102
Counterfactual exposure indices if those who entered into option schools through any choice program had remained at their local school	0.23605	0.21394	0.34607	0.24254	0.34083	0.26355
Net effect on exposure indices of all choice programs	0.00026	0.00205	0.00038	-0.00233	0.00327	-0.00253
Net effect on exposure indices of all choice programs (%)	0.11054	0.95832	0.11054	-0.95964	0.95832	-0.95964
Net effect of VEEP	0.00031	0.00109	0.00046	-0.00098	0.00174	-0.00106
Net effect of VEEP (%)	0.13282	0.51136	0.13282	-0.40229	0.51136	-0.40229
Net effect of magnet	0.00001	0.00064	0.00002	-0.00091	0.00103	-0.00099
Net effect of magnet (%)	0.00477	0.30079	0.00477	-0.37494	0.30079	-0.37494
Net effect of choice	-0.00009	0.00026	-0.00014	-0.00048	0.00042	-0.00053
Net effect of choice (%)	-0.03940	0.12316	-0.03940	-0.19968	0.12316	-0.19968

Table B.19

Districtwide Exposure Indices, by English-Learner Status

Exposure	EL to Non-EL	Non-EL to EL
Actual exposure indices in the district	0.54736	0.21915
Counterfactual exposure indices if those who entered into option schools through any choice program had remained at their local school	0.54860	0.21964
Net effect on exposure indices of all choice programs	–0.00124	–0.00050
Net effect on exposure indices of all choice programs (%)	–0.22602	–0.22602
Net effect of VEEP	0.00012	0.00005
Net effect of VEEP (%)	0.02244	0.02244
Net effect of magnet	–0.00073	–0.00029
Net effect of magnet (%)	–0.13317	–0.13317
Net effect of Choice	–0.00070	–0.00028
Net effect of Choice (%)	–0.12837	–0.12837

Appendix C

Methodology and Detailed Results on the Effect of Choice Programs on Outcomes

Definition of Lottery Groups, True Lotteries, and Fair Lotteries

For each of the VEEP, magnet, and open enrollment Choice programs, we had to separate applications into respective lotteries. These lotteries are defined by the school being applied to, the grade level, and the student's priority group. Roughly speaking, all three programs give top priority to students who already have a sibling in the school, followed by students who applied by or before March 1999 (before then, students were admitted on a first-come first-served basis), followed by students from SDUSD who applied during the 2000–2001 school year but before March 15.[1] Students who applied after March 15, 2001, were given the lowest priority and in addition were admitted on a first-come first-served basis. We therefore do not include this last group, because these students were not admitted by lottery. Siblings of current students, who themselves lived out of the district, followed by all other applicants from outside the district, constituted the final two lottery groups.

In addition, the magnet program separated students within each priority group into four clusters based on geographically contiguous

---

[1] Applications made after March 1999 but before the 2000–2001 school year were handled in the following way. The district had used a first-come first-served approach up until March 1999, in which applications that "lost" were held over for the next year. Beginning in the 1999–2000 school year, the district moved to a lottery system in which students who did not gain admission to their preferred school would have to apply again in the following year.

areas. The four clusters differ strongly in the racial/ethnic and socioeconomic makeup of resident students. These clusters were assigned a ranking for a given magnet from 1 to 4, such that the cluster with top priority least resembled the given magnet in racial/ethnic and socioeconomic characteristics and vice versa for the cluster with the lowest priority. For some magnet schools, applications were processed in strict order from cluster 1 to 4 or vice versa. For other magnets, fixed percentages of admittees had to be accepted from a given cluster. Within each cluster, priority groups were processed in order. On average, movements of students to magnets is thus expected to decrease racial/ethnic segregation at both the sending school and the magnet.[2]

The above description gives a concise summary of how lotteries were determined but is not entirely accurate for any of the three choice programs. There are a number of additional priority groups, such as "continuity," which refers to applications from magnet students to advance to a similar magnet in the next higher grade span and applications from students who are out of district. Appendix Table C.1 shows these priority groups, in descending priority order, for each program.

After sorting applicants into the schools and grades they applied to and the priority groups, we could thus identify the specific lottery into which they had been entered. We then identified true lotteries, by which we mean lotteries in which not all students won and not all students lost. It is essential that we focus only on these true lotteries because we need both winners and losers to populate our treatment and control groups, respectively. Although well over half of applications were to schools and grades that were oversubscribed, the subdivision of all these applications into various priority groups meant that quite often either all or none of the applications in a given group would be accepted, with only some priority groups admitting some but not all students. Table C.2 compares the number of lotteries to the number of true lotteries; the last

---

[2]Note, however, that within a school, all applicants to another school were treated equally regardless of race or ethnicity. Rather, the use of geographic clusters gives preference to *any* student at a school that is quite different in its racial/ethnic mix from the magnet school in question, relative to students at other schools that more closely resemble the magnet school in racial/ethnic terms.

Table C.1

Priority Groups and Number of Applications for Admission from Each Group, Fall 2001

Priority Group	2001–2002
VEEP	
(1) Sibling	164
(2) Before 9/3/99, from previous lists	1,231
(3) Received before 3/15 (in district)	3,037
(4) Received after 3/15 (in district)	3,662
(5) Out of district, received before 3/15	1
(6) Out of district, received after 3/15	4
Magnet	
(1) Sibling with continuity	56
(2) Continuity	360
(3) Sibling, received before 9/3/99	150
(4) Sibling	221
(5) Received before 9/3/99	6,552
(6) Received before 3/15	5,657
(7) Received after 3/15	4,055
(8) Out of district, before 9/3/99	198
(9) Out of district, received before 3/15	187
(10) Out of district, received after 3/15	185
Choice	
(1) Sibling	306
(2) Calendar change (no longer valid)	1,361
(3) Specialized course	117
(4) Received before 3/15 (in district)	5,303
(5) Received after 3/15 (in district)	4,778
(6) Out of district, received before 3/15	222
(7) Out of district, received after 3/15	618

NOTE: As indicated in the text, lotteries for magnets were further divided by students' geographic cluster.

column reduces the set of viable lotteries by dropping those in which test scores were missing in spring 2001, a year after the lottery, for all of the students who won, the students who lost, or both.[3]

---

[3]As expected there are generally no real lotteries with valid test scores for students entering kindergarten (grade 0) or grade 1, because the CST is first given to students in grade 2. There were a few minor exceptions and these were related mainly to students who skipped a grade or more after the lottery.

Table C.2

Lottery Counts for Unique Lotteries

Grade	Number of Lotteries	Number of True Lotteries	Number with CST Reading Scores
		VEEP	
0	60	2	0
1	38	1	0
2	42	4	4
3	46	5	5
4	48	6	5
5	44	1	1
6	34	11	11
7	25	13	13
8	24	10	10
9	22	10	10
10	20	5	5
11	20	4	4
12	17	4	2
Total	440	76	70
		Magnet	
0	160	23	0
1	115	24	2
2	121	24	24
3	106	23	22
4	98	19	19
5	101	16	15
6	101	13	13
7	67	11	11
8	51	10	10
9	85	21	21
10	63	17	15
11	48	7	7
12	36	5	2
Total	1,152	213	161
		Choice	
0	226	33	1
1	155	17	0
2	164	24	24
3	149	16	16
4	120	14	14
5	125	16	16
6	92	15	15

Table C.2 (continued)

Grade	Number of Lotteries	Number of True Lotteries	Number with CST Reading Scores
7	55	17	17
8	39	10	10
9	44	16	16
10	26	10	10
11	29	8	8
12	26	3	0
Total	1,250	199	147

Our next question was whether the true lotteries, which had both winners and losers, were fair in the sense that initial test scores of winners and losers were statistically indistinguishable. Although we report on an overall test of this in Chapter 4, we also felt that it was important to test this hypothesis for every regression reported in the text. After all, through attrition, the sample of students changes slightly each year. So, for example, suppose that within three years of the lottery, students with high achievement who lost the lottery were more likely to leave the district than were high-achieving students who won the lottery. This would bias our results in favor of the finding that school choice causally boosted test scores.

Table C.3 shows the results of these tests. For each corresponding regression of a test score in spring 2002, 2003, or 2004, we took the regression sample and regressed these students' spring 2001 test score in the corresponding test, from around the time of the lottery, on a set of lottery dummies (to allow for the fact that the average achievement of students applying to one school and grade was likely to differ from that of students in other lotteries), plus a dummy to indicate lottery winners. The hypothesis that the remaining subsample was balanced was checked by testing whether the coefficient on the dummy variable for lottery winners was zero.

Recall that all test scores were rescaled to have a mean of zero and a standard deviation of one within each grade in the district. Typically, the coefficients on the dummy for lottery winners is small and insignificant. In 15 cases out of 178 regressions, the lottery winner

Table C.3

Tests for Identical Prelottery Test Scores Between Lottery Winners and Losers, for Each Regression Sample and Year

Test Year	Test	Reading			Math		
		VEEP	Magnet	Choice	VEEP	Magnet	Choice
All Grade Spans							
2002	CST	−0.0759	0.0148	−0.0621	−0.0520	−0.0141	−0.0443
	Stanford 9	−0.1013	−0.0054	−0.0468	−0.0698	0.0078	0.0063
	SDRT	−0.0479	0.0333	−0.0551			
2003	CST	−0.0992	0.0148	−0.0626	−0.0874	−0.0311	−0.0080
	CAT/6	−0.1226*	−0.0054	−0.0285	−0.1014	−0.0135	0.0343
	SDRT	−0.0457	0.0333	−0.0774			
2004	CST	−0.0987	0.0173	−0.0757	−0.0553	−0.0577	−0.0105
	CAT/6	−0.1337*	−0.0194	−0.0480	−0.1006	−0.0287	0.0275
	SDRT	−0.0752	−0.0246	−0.1285			
Elementary School Grade Spans							
2002	CST	−0.1306	−0.0633	−0.0704	−0.5259	−0.0968	−0.0539
	Stanford 9	−0.1808	−0.1230	0.0104	−0.4710	−0.0939	0.0170
	SDRT	0.2705	0.0849	−0.1401			
2003	CST	−0.0542	−0.1725	0.0094	−0.5222	−0.2635	0.0533
	CAT/6	−0.2033	−0.2203	0.1648	−0.6075	−0.2692*	0.1074
	SDRT	0.1027	0.0857	−0.1311			
2004	CST	−0.4422	−0.0668	0.0110	−0.7122	−0.2909*	0.0026
	CAT/6	−0.4019	−0.1830	0.1891	−0.7154	−0.2753	0.0869
	SDRT	0.1534	−0.0907	0.0626			
Middle School Grade Spans							
2002	CST	−0.0992	0.0794	−0.1523	−0.0671	0.1000	−0.1940*
	Stanford 9	−0.1360*	0.0926	−0.1595*	−0.1156	0.0673	−0.2014*
	SDRT	−0.0478	−0.0046	−0.1426			
2003	CST	−0.1149	0.0814	−0.1195	−0.0958	0.1357	−0.1798
	CAT/6	−0.1381*	0.1087	−0.1374	−0.1290*	0.0965	−0.1568
	SDRT	−0.0379	0.0327	−0.1403			
2004	CST	−0.1139	0.0721	−0.1460	−0.0675	0.0630	−0.1653
	CAT/6	−0.1532*	0.0722	−0.1653	−0.1204	0.0621	−0.1666
	SDRT	−0.0740	−0.0140	−0.1544			
High School Grade Spans							
2002	CST	0.1114	−0.0155	0.0874	0.1885	−0.0670	0.1615
	Stanford 9	0.1086	−0.0426	0.0977	0.2212	−0.0268	0.2634**
	SDRT	0.0097	0.1315	0.0761			
2003	CST	0.0327	0.0165	0.0246	0.1243	−0.0723	0.2041
	CAT/6	0.0043	−0.0068	0.0841	0.1283	−0.0064	0.2830*
	SDRT	−0.0082	−0.0252	0.0321			

Table C.3 (continued)

Test Year	Test	Reading			Math		
		VEEP	Magnet	Choice	VEEP	Magnet	Choice
2004	CST	0.1845	−0.0443	0.0407	0.3418	−0.1376	0.2784*
	CAT/6	0.1452	−0.0392	0.0705	0.2124	−0.0685	0.3134*
	SDRT		0.6403				

NOTES: Each cell refers to the coefficient for the dummy indicating whether the student won the given lottery. Each regression models the test score (with mean zero and standard deviation one districtwide, for each grade and year) in spring 2001, before lottery results were announced, as a function of the dummy for having won a lottery. All models contain fixed effects for the specific lottery and a random effect for the actual school attended in 2000–2001. The regression sample is from specification (1) of the corresponding models in Appendix Tables C.4 through C.9. However, when we model spring 2001 achievement, the sample sizes drop somewhat below specification (1) to the sample sizes seen for models (2) and higher in Chapter 4, because not all students had spring 2001 test scores available. For the math samples, we model spring 2001 math test scores, and for the reading samples we model the 2001 reading scores.

*Significantly different from zero at the 5 percent level.

**Significantly different from zero at the 1 percent level.

variable was significant at 5 percent or less, and in only one case was it significant at 1 percent or less. To put this in perspective, if lottery winners and losers in each of the samples truly had the same underlying 2001 achievement level, we would still find 5 percent of the coefficients significant at the 5 percent level and 1 percent at the 1 percent level. We find something quite close to this, with 8.4 percent and 0.6 percent significant at these levels, respectively.

Thus, although these results suggest that there was no significant selectivity bias in the samples of winners and losers, we should take care in the cases in which we did find at least a mildly significant coefficient. These tended to be in middle school and high school and more often in math than in reading. In these cases, it suggests that a close comparison of specifications (1) and (2) are in order in the test-score models: If the samples were slightly unequal in initial achievement, then the addition of a lagged test score in specifications (2) and higher could potentially make some statistically significant coefficients on lottery winners fall back into insignificance.

Econometric Specification and Interpretation

Consider how we test for the effect of winning a lottery for any one of the three choice programs—VEEP, magnet, or Choice. We identify lotteries that are "true" in the sense that not all applicants win and not all lose. Assume that there are J of these lotteries. We will model the test score for student i in year t, where t is one of the postlottery years 2002, 2003, or 2004. This student applies to lottery j, and in year t attends school s, so his score is denoted by S_{ijst}. We model this test score as a function of a set of dummy variables α_j for the lottery applied to, a dummy variable WIN_{ijt} and corresponding coefficient β indicating whether the student i, whose test score is modeled in year t, won lottery j, and a composite error term in parentheses consisting of an error component for school s in year t, η_{st}, and a white noise error term ε_{ijst}:

$$S_{ijst} = \sum_{j=1}^{J} \alpha_j + \beta WIN_{ijt} + \left(\eta_{st} + \varepsilon_{ijst} \right).$$

We estimate this as a random effect model to account for grouping of students in school s in the given year t.

We actually estimate five main specifications, in addition to specification (1) listed above. In specifications (2) and (3), we add the spring 2001 test score in the same subject. This can often improve the precision of the estimates because, although a lottery may be fair, this is not the same as saying that in the actual sample initial test scores are exactly identical (Donner and Klar, 2000; Bloom, 2003). In any finite sample, this will almost never be the case. The addition of a lagged test score, squared, in specification (3) is likely to be more important in the models that use the CST, because as a criterion-referenced test, it is not vertically scaled. The quadratic in initial 2001 achievement allows for a nonlinear relation between 2001 and later test scores. In specification (4), we control for additional personal characteristics. One can think of this as an additional test showing that random variations in student characteristics between the lottery winners and lottery losers are not driving results. Finally, in specification (5), we add controls for school and classroom characteristics, such as class size and teacher qualifications. In cases where lottery winners appear to have higher test scores after winning the lottery, it is interesting to see if this difference can be explained by differences in the school and classroom environments of lottery winners and losers.

It is important to distinguish between two closely related hypotheses. What the randomization allows us to do convincingly is to estimate the effect of winning a lottery. Social scientists refer to this as the "effect of the offer to treat" or more simply the effect of the "intent to treat." But winning a lottery to attend a certain school is not the same as winning a lottery to attend that school, accepting the offer, and actually attending. The overall effect on winners who switch is known as the effect of "treatment on the treated." It is far more difficult to estimate the latter, because those winners who choose to attend the school are likely to be a self-selected group of students with a higher-than-average desire to leave their current school. Compared to lottery winners who ultimately decide to decline the offer, they may be either more or less likely to have high test scores in subsequent years. For instance, those who accept the offer may be more motivated than average, so that they would have higher test-score gains. Conversely, those families that accept may be particularly desperate to improve the rate of learning of the student in question, so that on average those who accept the offer might have lower test-score gains. The implication is that if we restricted the analysis to winners who actually left, we might severely overestimate or underestimate the actual causal effect of winning the lottery. This same concern remains if we, for instance, model the effect of winning a lottery and switching schools on test scores after using instrumental variables to predict the probability that winners switch, using the proportion of applicants who won the lottery as an instrument. We are in the early stages of studying whether it will be feasible to estimate accurately the effect of treatment. Results throughout the literature on experimental evaluation of training programs suggest that this will prove difficult (see, for instance, Heckman, 1997, and section 5 of Heckman, Lalonde, and Smith, 1999, for a detailed discussion of the technical issues).

Regression Results for All Specifications

Below we present six tables that show the regression coefficients underlying Tables 4.2 and 4.3 in Chapter 4. These tables are more detailed than those in Chapter 4 because they show all of the specifications for each test, running from the simplest model that conditions only on dummies for the specific lottery up to the most complex model that conditions current-year test score on lottery dummies, a quadratic in initial test scores, as well as personal characteristics and characteristics of the student's classroom.[4]

Some of the results in these tables, and in particular variations across specifications, deserve mention. For example, specification (1), which does not control for initial test scores, sometimes produces results suggesting that winning a given lottery was associated with higher or lower subsequent achievement. For example, in Appendix Table C.4, three out of six versions of specification (1) for VEEP middle school reading show significant negative effects of winning a lottery. But these negative effects in middle school reading in year 1 are less robust than might appear. The tests for equal prelottery test scores in Appendix Table C.3 indeed show that for the middle school results for Stanford 9 in 2002 and CAT/6 in 2003 the initial (prelottery) test scores of lottery winners were significantly lower. This probably explains why the apparently negative effects of VEEP from specification (1) in both cases become insignificant in specification (2).

Similarly, in Appendix Table C.6, at the high school level for magnet applicants, none of the models of reading achievement shows a significant coefficient for lottery winners, except for CST reading scores in 2003, which, according to specification (1), are about 0.2 of a standard deviation higher for lottery winners. However, the more complex models that condition on prelottery reading scores do not show such an effect.

---

[4]We also present summary statistics on our data and full regression results in tables available in Appendix E, a web-only appendix available at http://www.ppic.org/content/other/806JBR_web_only_appendix.pdf. That web appendix contains 30 detailed tables. The first six show summary statistics and the final 24 show regression results in more detail. The ordering of the latter tables follows that of Chapter 4 loosely, with four sets of tables showing results for the all grade spans sample, followed by the elementary, middle, and high school samples. Within each of these sets, we show results for VEEP reading and math in two tables, followed by four other tables in the same order of reading and math, for magnets and Choice.

Again, in the math results for the Choice program, we sometimes find that adding control variables for initial test scores or personal characteristics makes significant results either become smaller or become insignificant altogether. Appendix Table C.9 shows the relevant results. In many cases, apparently significant results in specification (1) are not robust. As mentioned in Chapter 4, in middle schools in 2002, lottery winners scored below lottery losers on the CST. However, even here, the test for identical prelottery test scores suggested that in this sample, pre-lottery test scores were lower for lottery winners. Indeed, specifications (2) and (3), which condition on this prelottery test score, show smaller but still significant effects. Also, in specification (4), where we add a host of personal characteristics, this effect disappears, which suggests that other differences between the lottery and winners could account for any differences, rather than the Choice program itself. Similarly, another negative result for middle school lottery winners, this time in 2004 CAT/6 results, disappears after controlling for prelottery test scores. For high schools, we find numerous models suggesting that lottery winners had higher test scores, but as shown in Appendix Table C.3 above, many of these models had samples for which lottery winners had significantly higher *prelottery* test scores. It is thus unsurprising that in specifiction (2) and later, which condition on prelottery achievement, there is no significant difference between lottery winners' and losers' math achievement in later years.

Table C.4

Estimated Effects of Winning a VEEP Lottery on Reading Scores on Various Measures of Reading Achievement, and for Various Specifications, Spring 2002 Through Spring 2004

Test Year	Test	Specification (1)	(2)	(3)	(4)	(5)
		All Grade Spans				
2002	CST	−0.1227*	−0.0994**	−0.0979**	−0.1002**	−0.0933
	Stanford 9	−0.1420*	−0.0872*	−0.0870*	−0.0865*	−0.0903
	SDRT	−0.0542	−0.0839*	−0.0804*	−0.0860*	−0.0476
2003	CST	−0.0987	−0.0575	−0.0624	−0.0649	−0.0821
	CAT/6	−0.1022	−0.0595	−0.0600	−0.0842	−0.0862
	SDRT	−0.0887	−0.0490	−0.0424	−0.0559	−0.0866
2004	CST	−0.0539	0.0055	0.0003	−0.0086	−0.0188
	CAT/6	−0.0622	−0.0065	−0.0064	−0.0345	−0.0580
	SDRT	−0.1233	−0.0898	−0.0853	−0.0959	−0.1173
		Elementary School Grade Spans				
2002	CST	0.0069	0.0645	0.0429	−0.0219	
	Stanford 9	−0.0911	0.1301	0.1103	−0.0543	
	SDRT	0.2705				
2003	CST	−0.2024	−0.1617	−0.2104		
	CAT/6	0.3723	0.4441*	0.3854		
	SDRT	0.1027				
2004	CST	0.2357	0.5353*	0.5316*		
	CAT/6	0.0153	0.2512	0.2462		
	SDRT	0.1534				
		Middle School Grade Spans				
2002	CST	−0.1375*	−0.0868*	−0.0848*	−0.0868*	−0.0780
	Stanford 9	−0.1453*	−0.0678	−0.0685	−0.0756	−0.0631
	SDRT	−0.0896	−0.0980*	−0.0940*	−0.0986*	−0.0498
2003	CST	−0.0829	−0.0157	−0.0151	−0.0454	−0.0679
	CAT/6	−0.1391*	−0.0628	−0.0637	−0.0925	−0.1011
	SDRT	−0.0825	−0.0605	−0.0582	−0.0588	−0.0981
2004	CST	−0.1040	−0.0222	−0.0215	−0.0405	−0.0711
	CAT/6	−0.1165	−0.0384	−0.0370	−0.0503	−0.0943
	SDRT	−0.1314	−0.0902	−0.0855	−0.0958	−0.1174
		High School Grade Spans				
2002	CST	−0.1524	−0.1915*	−0.1921*	−0.1720*	−0.1969
	Stanford 9	−0.1275	−0.1839*	−0.1955**	−0.1825*	−0.2087
	SDRT	0.0055	0.0050	−0.0008	0.0236	−0.0008
2003	CST	−0.0885	−0.1081	−0.1140	−0.0916	−0.0750
	CAT/6	−0.1028	−0.1262	−0.1242	−0.1412	−0.1418
	SDRT	−0.1028	−0.1262	−0.1242	−0.1412	0.1799

Table C.4 (continued)

Test Year	Test	Specification (1)	(2)	(3)	(4)	(5)
2004	CST	0.1668	0.0844	0.0810	0.1201	0.1184
	CAT/6	0.1855	0.0043	−0.0180	0.1233	0.1894
	SDRT					

Other Regressors					
Grade dummies	Yes	Yes	Yes	Yes	Yes
2001 test score		Yes	Yes	Yes	Yes
2001 test score squared			Yes	Yes	Yes
Personal controls				Yes	Yes
Classroom controls					Yes

NOTES: Each cell refers to the coefficient for the dummy indicating whether the student won the given lottery. Each regression models the test score (with mean zero and standard deviation one districtwide, for each grade and year) as a function of the dummy for having won a lottery. All models contain fixed effects for the specific lottery and a random effect for the actual school attended.

*Significantly different from zero at the 5 percent level.

**Significantly different from zero at the 1 percent level.

Table C.5

Estimated Effects of Winning a VEEP Lottery on Math Scores on Various Measures of Math Achievement, by Grade Span and for Various Specifications, Spring 2002 Through Spring 2004

Test Year	Test	Specification				
		(1)	(2)	(3)	(4)	(5)
All Grade Spans						
2002	CST	−0.0909	−0.0730	−0.0802*	−0.0733	−0.0716
	Stanford 9	−0.0673	−0.0257	−0.0248	−0.0229	−0.0387
2003	CST	−0.0186	0.0197	0.0060	−0.0104	−0.0278
	CAT/6	−0.0846	−0.0063	−0.0068	−0.0083	−0.0252
2004	CST	−0.0127	−0.0304	−0.0325	−0.0388	−0.0631
	CAT/6	−0.0217	0.0184	0.0087	0.0049	−0.0330
Elementary School Grade Spans						
2002	CST	−0.3364	−0.0378	0.0098	−0.4348*	
	Stanford 9	−0.3266	0.0449	0.0402	−0.3385	
2003	CST	−0.3471	−0.0648	−0.0185		
	CAT/6	−0.2962	0.2194	0.2116		
2004	CST	−0.1076	0.1289	0.3889		
	CAT/6	−0.0447	0.1566	0.0506		
Middle School Grade Spans						
2002	CST	−0.1077	−0.1035*	−0.1114*	−0.0970*	−0.0974
	Stanford 9	−0.0833	−0.0327	−0.0317	−0.0281	−0.0331
2003	CST	−0.0178	0.0247	0.0179	−0.0052	0.0092
	CAT/6	−0.0857	−0.0156	−0.0181	−0.0236	−0.0421
2004	CST	−0.0432	−0.0336	−0.0405	−0.0363	−0.0591
	CAT/6	−0.0558	−0.0073	−0.0091	−0.0150	−0.0562
High School Grade Spans						
2002	CST	0.2098	0.0695	0.0644	0.0483	0.0154
	Stanford 9	0.1699	0.0011	−0.0144	−0.0484	−0.0733
2003	CST	0.0449	−0.0204	−0.0336	−0.0484	−0.0985
	CAT/6	0.1790	−0.0055	−0.0098	0.0247	0.0383
2004	CST	0.0747	−0.0296	−0.0020	−0.0130	−0.1118
	CAT/6	0.3450	0.1008	0.0745	0.0425	0.1951
Other Regressors						
Grade dummies		Yes	Yes	Yes	Yes	Yes
2001 test score			Yes	Yes	Yes	Yes
2001 test score squared				Yes	Yes	Yes
Personal controls					Yes	Yes
Classroom controls						Yes

NOTE: See the notes to Table C.4.

Table C.6

Estimated Effects of Winning a Magnet Lottery on Reading Scores on Various Measures of Reading Achievement, by Grade Span and for Various Specifications, Spring 2002 Through Spring 2004

Test Year	Test	Specification				
		(1)	(2)	(3)	(4)	(5)
All Grade Spans						
2002	CST	0.0181	0.0497	0.0467	0.0481	0.0451
	Stanford 9	−0.0127	0.0753*	0.0746*	0.0743*	0.0469
	SDRT	−0.0331	0.0299	0.0302	0.0257	0.0204
2003	CST	−0.0231	0.0602	0.0567	0.0359	0.0122
	CAT/6	0.0245	0.0858	0.0830	0.0563	0.0375
	SDRT	−0.0139	0.0492	0.0492	0.0544	0.0079
2004	CST	−0.0592	0.0578	0.0522	0.0160	−0.0201
	CAT/6	−0.0650	0.0031	0.0028	−0.0274	−0.0879
	SDRT	−0.1519	0.0295	0.0295	−0.0015	0.0170
Elementary School Grade Spans						
2002	CST	−0.0576	−0.0259	−0.0318	−0.0069	−0.0106
	Stanford 9	−0.0613	0.1383	0.1404	0.1095	0.0289
	SDRT	−0.0433	0.1417	0.1755	0.2105*	0.2211
2003	CST	−0.1596	0.0107	0.0023	0.0439	0.0253
	CAT/6	−0.0565	0.1452	0.1355	0.1688	0.2087
	SDRT	0.0346	0.3170*	0.3093*	0.3700**	
2004	CST	−0.1934**	−0.0949	−0.0906	−0.0936	−0.0705
	CAT/6	−0.1647*	−0.0779	−0.0798	−0.0903	−0.0903
	SDRT	−0.2770*	0.1088	0.0793	0.0746	
Middle School Grade Spans						
2002	CST	−0.0105	0.0094	0.0083	−0.0023	0.0097
	Stanford 9	−0.0347	0.0034	−0.0057	−0.0110	−0.0402
	SDRT	−0.1341	−0.0305	−0.0310	−0.0427	−0.0227
2003	CST	0.0067	−0.0173	−0.0213	−0.0208	−0.0409
	CAT/6	−0.0038	−0.0149	−0.0218	−0.0168	−0.0170
	SDRT	−0.0228	−0.0228	−0.0235	−0.0533	−0.0756
2004	CST	0.0547	0.0399	0.0313	−0.0213	0.0216
	CAT/6	−0.0665	−0.0612	−0.0714	−0.0871	−0.1292
	SDRT	−0.0631	0.0181	0.0185	−0.0050	−0.0051
High School Grade Spans						
2002	CST	0.1793	0.0893	0.0795	0.0704	0.0687
	Stanford 9	0.1133	0.0683	0.0640	0.0649	0.0272
	SDRT	0.1095	0.0327	0.0328	0.0418	0.0134

Table C.6 (continued)

Test Year	Test	Specification (1)	(2)	(3)	(4)	(5)
2003	CST	0.2247*	0.0978	0.0905	0.0945	0.1186
	CAT/6	0.1870	0.0854	0.0845	0.0468	0.0419
	SDRT	0.0386	0.0620	0.0611	0.1109	0.0548
2004	CST	0.0895	0.0261	0.0059	−0.0055	0.0066
	CAT/6	0.1373	0.0269	−0.0019	−0.0629	−0.0547
	SDRT	0.6403				
Other Regressors						
Grade dummies		Yes	Yes	Yes	Yes	Yes
2001 test score			Yes	Yes	Yes	Yes
2001 test score squared				Yes	Yes	Yes
Personal controls					Yes	Yes
Classroom controls						Yes

NOTE: See the notes to Table C.4.

Table C.7

Estimated Effects of Winning a Magnet Lottery on Math Scores on Various Measures of Math Achievement, by Grade Span and for Various Specifications, Spring 2002 Through Spring 2004

Test Year	Test	Specification (1)	(2)	(3)	(4)	(5)
		All Grade Spans				
2002	CST	−0.0402	−0.0192	−0.0174	−0.0155	−0.0036
	Stanford 9	−0.0698	−0.0362	−0.0363	−0.0385	−0.0399
2003	CST	0.0162	0.1235*	0.1248**	0.1172*	0.1118
	CAT/6	0.0063	0.0234	0.0256	0.0305	0.0771
2004	CST	−0.0682	0.0661	0.0577	0.0459	0.0414
	CAT/6	−0.0262	0.0990	0.1020	0.0944	0.0278
		Elementary School Grade Spans				
2002	CST	−0.1149	−0.0717	−0.0644	−0.0586	−0.0404
	Stanford 9	−0.1847	−0.1317	−0.1277	−0.1202	−0.1147
2003	CST	−0.1385	0.0128	0.0218	0.0399	0.0889
	CAT/6	−0.1083	0.0886	0.0769	0.0936	0.1168
2004	CST	−0.0962	−0.0460	−0.0554	−0.0595	0.1018
	CAT/6	−0.1011	−0.0098	−0.0039	0.0251	0.0078
		Middle School Grade Spans				
2002	CST	−0.0058	−0.0270	−0.0263	−0.0337	−0.0202
	Stanford 9	−0.0210	−0.0165	−0.0187	−0.0439	−0.0343
2003	CST	0.0202	0.0133	0.0187	0.0228	−0.0598
	CAT/6	−0.0339	−0.0652	−0.0550	−0.0667	−0.0236
2004	CST	−0.1483	−0.1359	−0.1376	−0.1295	−0.0680
	CAT/6	0.0558	0.0353	0.0419	−0.0364	0.0234
		High School Grade Spans				
2002	CST	0.0252	−0.0255	−0.0225	−0.0091	0.0131
	Stanford 9	0.0228	−0.0277	−0.0267	−0.0185	−0.0230
2003	CST	0.1688	0.1824*	0.1835*	0.2284*	0.2657
	CAT/6	0.0739	0.0155	0.0185	0.0471	0.0545
2004	CST	0.2374	0.2308*	0.2261*	0.1748	0.2725
	CAT/6	0.1113	0.0849	0.0949	0.1264	0.1118
Other Regressors						
Grade dummies		Yes	Yes	Yes	Yes	Yes
2001 test score			Yes	Yes	Yes	Yes
2001 test score squared				Yes	Yes	Yes
Personal controls					Yes	Yes
Classroom controls						Yes

NOTE: See the notes to Table C.4.

Table C.8

Estimated Effects of Winning a Choice Lottery on Reading Scores on Various Measures of Reading Achievement, by Grade Span and for Various Specifications, Spring 2002 Through Spring 2004

Test Year	Test	Specification (1)	(2)	(3)	(4)	(5)
		All Grade Spans				
2002	CST	−0.0394	0.0215	0.0189	0.0252	0.0341
	Stanford 9	−0.0290	−0.0173	−0.0134	−0.0061	−0.0050
	SDRT	−0.0368	−0.0172	−0.0131	0.0034	0.0063
2003	CST	−0.0457	0.0294	0.0223	0.0290	−0.0480
	CAT/6	−0.0416	−0.0397	−0.0306	−0.0198	−0.0469
	SDRT	−0.0404	−0.0098	−0.0217	−0.0424	−0.0489
2004	CST	−0.0386	−0.0319	−0.0370	−0.0251	−0.0493
	CAT/6	−0.0135	−0.1036*	−0.1049*	−0.0922	−0.1049
	SDRT	−0.1286	−0.1915**	−0.1878**	−0.1476*	−0.1412
		Elementary School Grade Spans				
2002	CST	0.1250	0.0406	0.0124	0.0062	−0.0006
	Stanford 9	0.1505	−0.0010	0.0211	0.0084	−0.0590
	SDRT	0.1025	−0.0924	−0.0661	0.0472	
2003	CST	−0.0184	−0.0231	−0.0423	−0.0818	−0.1268
	CAT/6	−0.0352	−0.1996	−0.1675	−0.1812	−0.1224
	SDRT	0.0515	−0.1318	−0.1553	−0.0354	
2004	CST	0.0775	−0.1639	−0.1931	−0.0251	−0.3124
	CAT/6	0.0844	−0.3013**	−0.3065**	−0.3113**	−0.3339
	SDRT	0.0970	−0.6047**	−0.6305**	−0.6509**	
		Middle School Grade Spans				
2002	CST	−0.1715	−0.0010	0.0025	0.0037	0.0029
	Stanford 9	−0.1713	−0.0319	−0.0345	−0.0357	−0.0250
	SDRT	−0.1178	−0.0544	−0.0504	−0.0505	−0.0408
2003	CST	−0.1684	−0.0212	−0.0116	−0.0850	−0.0397
	CAT/6	−0.1381	0.0273	0.0174	0.0180	0.0182
	SDRT	−0.1509	−0.1042	−0.1216*	−0.1377**	−0.1477
2004	CST	0.2374	0.2308*	0.2261*	0.1748	0.2725
	CAT/6	0.1113	0.0849	0.0949	0.1264	0.1118
	SDRT	−0.2696*	−0.1426*	−0.1380	−0.1200*	−0.1190
		High School Grade Spans				
2002	CST	0.1183	0.0032	−0.0050	−0.0148	−0.0191
	Stanford 9	0.1631	0.040	0.0367	0.0210	0.0150
	SDRT	0.1466	0.0851	0.0977	0.0792	0.0602
2003	CST	0.1519	0.0129	−0.0033	−0.0253	0.0605
	CAT/6	0.1003	−0.1075	−0.1155	−0.0952	−0.0103
	SDRT	0.0887	0.1459*	0.1628**	0.169	0.1194

Table C.8 (continued)

Test Year	Test	Specification (1)	(2)	(3)	(4)	(5)
2004	CST	−0.0350	0.0370	0.0101	−0.0251	−0.0099
	CAT/6	−0.0772	−0.1111	−0.1256	−0.1450	−0.0720
	SDRT					

Other Regressors					
Grade dummies	Yes	Yes	Yes	Yes	Yes
2001 test score		Yes	Yes	Yes	Yes
2001 test score squared			Yes	Yes	Yes
Personal controls				Yes	Yes
Classroom controls					Yes

NOTE: See the notes to Table C.4.

Table C.9

Estimated Effects of Winning a Choice Lottery on Math Scores on Various Measures of Math Achievement, by Grade Span and for Various Specifications, Spring 2002 Through Spring 2004

Test Year	Test	Specification				
		(1)	(2)	(3)	(4)	(5)
All Grade Spans						
2002	CST	−0.0451	−0.0247	−0.0228	−0.0161	−0.0060
	Stanford 9	0.0136	−0.0438	−0.0436	−0.0315	−0.0231
2003	CST	0.0042	−0.0175	−0.0150	−0.0031	0.0072
	CAT/6	−0.0449	−0.0380	−0.0342	−0.0242	−0.0500
2004	CST	−0.0174	−0.1078	−0.1133	−0.1131	−0.1321
	CAT/6	−0.0562	−0.0516	−0.0444	−0.0300	−0.0392
Elementary School Grade Spans						
2002	CST	0.0057	−0.0472	−0.0658	−0.0428	0.0122
	Stanford 9	0.1127	−0.0126	−0.0042	−0.0009	0.0247
2003	CST	−0.0609	−0.1247	−0.1358	−0.1679	−0.1327
	CAT/6	−0.0206	−0.0120	−0.0022	−0.0156	−0.0994
2004	CST	0.1015	−0.0522	−0.1229	−0.1596	−0.3200
	CAT/6	−0.0278	−0.0542	−0.0606	−0.0819	−0.0953
Middle School Grade Spans						
2002	CST	−0.2662**	−0.1678**	−0.1699**	−0.0826	−0.1002
	Stanford 9	−0.1518	−0.0694	−0.0696	−0.0394	−0.0356
2003	CST	−0.0387	0.0208	0.0242	0.0366	0.0699
	CAT/6	−0.1390	−0.0706	−0.0699	−0.0878	−0.0946
2004	CST	−0.2420*	−0.1864	−0.1735	−0.1188	−0.0935
	CAT/6	−0.2055	−0.0730	−0.0172	−0.0166	−0.0214
High School Grade Spans						
2002	CST	0.2458**	0.1021	0.0975	0.0854	0.0705
	Stanford 9	0.2397*	−0.0014	−0.0042	−0.0081	0.0039
2003	CST	0.2656*	0.0033	−0.0311	−0.0254	0.0606
	CAT/6	0.2176*	−0.0400	−0.0240	−0.0317	0.0112
2004	CST	0.0854	−0.0110	−0.0309	−0.1010	−0.1678
	CAT/6	0.0856	−0.0696	−0.0772	−0.0951	−0.0663

Other Regressors					
Grade dummies	Yes	Yes	Yes	Yes	Yes
2001 test score		Yes	Yes	Yes	Yes
2001 test score squared			Yes	Yes	Yes
Personal controls				Yes	Yes
Classroom controls					Yes

NOTE: See the notes to Table C.4.

Appendix D

Supplementary Information Related to Charter Schools

Table D.1
Correlation Table of Survey Responses

	Average Daily Attendance, 2003–2004	Year in Operation, 2003–2004	School Operates in a			Major Challenge Facing the School		
			Church	Traditional School Building	Office Building	Finances	Facilities	Lack of Parental Involvement
Average daily attendance, 2003–2004	1							
Year of operation, 2003–2004	0.52	1						
School operates in a								
Church	-0.49	-0.14	1					
Traditional school building	0.73	0.73	-0.59	1				
Office building	-0.22	-0.62	-0.51	-0.39	1			
Finances are a problem	0.25	0.02	-0.22	-0.02	0.28	1		
Facilities are a problem	-0.24	-0.27	-0.07	-0.23	0.33	-0.28	1	
Lack of parental involvement is a problem	-0.07	0.16	0.42	-0.03	-0.45	0.29	-0.45	1

	Target Students	School Actively Targets According to				% Local
		Area	LEP Status	Disadvantaged	At-Risk	
Target students	1					
Students living in particular area	0.38	1				
Limited English-proficient students	0.66	0.7	1			
Disadvantaged students	1	0.38	0.66	1		
At-risk students	0.37	0.55	0.55	0.37	1	
% of students from local attendance area	-0.59	-0.4	-0.31	-0.59	-0.43	1

Table D.1 (continued)

	Longer Day	Longer Year	Instruction Days	Waitlist	Random Lottery	Union	% of Teachers from SDUSD
Longer school day	1						
Longer school year	0.26	1					
Instruction days	0.33	0.7	1				
School has waitlist	0.2	-0.45	-0.45	1			
School holds a random lottery	0.34	0.04	-0.18	0.47	1		
Teachers are subject to collective bargaining agreement	-0.53	0.08	-0.15	-0.17	-0.47	1	
% of teachers from district	-0.26	0.13	-0.31	-0.18	-0.12	0.31	1

	Number of Parent-Teacher Mandatory Meetings	Number of Parent-Teacher Meetings	Number of Mandatory Parent Hours	Number of Parent Hours	Parents Sign Learning Contract	Parent Involvement Is Problem
Number of parent-teacher mandatory meetings	1					
Number of parent-teacher meetings	0.22	1				
Number of mandatory parent service hours	0.31	0.04	1			
Number of hours parents volunteer a year	0.32	-0.26	0.33	1		
Parents sign learning contract	0.53	0.4	-0.32	-0.25	1	
Parent involvement is a problem	0.22	0.3	-0.46	-0.19	0.41	1

Table D.2

Stanford 9 Test-Score Gain Regression Coefficients on Charter School Indicator

	Student Fixed Effects OLS	Sample Sizes		Anderson-Hsiao IV	Sample Sizes	
		Number of Students [Number of Observations]	Number of Charter Students		Number of Students [Number of Observations]	Number of Charter Students
Elementary School						
Math	-7.6837 (2.2194)**	62,795 [111,313]	1,524	-6.4625 (1.4783)**	34,023 [48,484]	768
Reading	-3.567 (2.0000)	61,036 [107,116]	1,489	-3.4854 (1.6841)*	32,702 [46,048]	737
Middle School						
Math	2.47 (0.7303)**	56,172 [100,211]	5,898	1.4758 (0.3816)**	41,050 [67,680]	4,329
Reading	-3.0934 (0.7173)**	55,793 [98,882]	5,810	-2.5034 (0.4074)**	40,181 [65,706]	4,181
High School						
Math	-0.3107 (0.9234)	47,674 [84,101]	3,176	-3.3482 (0.4391)**	34,459 [56,134]	1,947
Reading	1.1219 (0.7989)	47,304 [83,169]	3,135	0.4856 (0.3778)	34,112 [55,459]	1,896

NOTES: All estimates include year and grade fixed effects. Standard errors are in parentheses. The dependent variable is Stanford 9 test-score gain.

*Significant at the 5 percent level.

**Significant at the 1 percent level.

Stanford 9 Test-Score Gain Regression Coefficients on Charter School Type Indicators

		Student Fixed Effects OLS	Anderson-Hsiao IV
Elementary School			
Math	Charter	−6.8158	−7.0437
		(2.6970)*	(1.7899)**
	Conversion charter	−2.6216	1.7796
		(4.6285)	(3.0904)
	p-value (charter + conversion)	0.0132	0.0392
Reading	Charter	−2.4397	−3.1629
		(2.4087)	(2.0186)
	Conversion charter	−3.5305	−1.0292
		(4.2034)	(3.5527)
	p-value (charter + conversion)	0.0872	0.1573
Middle School			
Math	Charter	−0.6462	0.4117
		(1.4033)	(0.7236)
	Conversion charter	4.0915	1.422
		(1.5734)**	(0.8224)
	p-value (charter + conversion)	0.0000	0.0000
Reading	Charter	1.2482	0.0013
		(1.3623)	(0.7675)
	Conversion charter	−5.7536	−3.3758
		(1.5349)**	(0.8761)**
	p-value (charter + conversion)	0.0000	0.0000

NOTES: All estimates include year and grade fixed effects. Because there are no conversion high schools, the results in Appendix Table D.2 fully capture results for startup charter high schools. The p-value provides the level of significance for a test that the charter and conversion variables both equal zero. This provides a test of whether conversions are identical to regular public schools. Standard errors are in parentheses.

*Significant at the 5 percent level.

**Significant at the 1 percent level.

Table D.4

Stanford 9 Test-Score Gain Regression Coefficients, Year in Operation

		Calculated with Student Fixed Effects OLS	p-value (charter + X)
		Elementary School	
Math	Charter	3.4104 (3.5330)	
	Conversion	−12.9473 (5.1660)*	0.0123
	1st year	−25.7978 (5.4819)**	0.0000
	2nd year	−6.8796 (3.7982)	0.3293
	3rd year	−15.055 (3.6034)**	0.002
Reading	Charter	4.0684 (3.1585)	
	Conversion	−10.1279 (4.6799)*	0.0826
	1st year	−12.6611 (4.8728)**	0.0378
	2nd year	−7.5121 (3.3719)*	0.2772
	3rd year	−9.6153 (3.2443)**	0.0972
		Middle School	
Math	Charter	−2.4711 (1.5486)	
	Conversion	5.9541 (1.7091)**	0.0000
	1st year	−7.0906 (5.6752)	0.0831
	2nd year	9.9954 (2.9752)**	0.009
	3rd year	10.6459 (3.1536)**	0.007
Reading	Charter	1.9183 (1.4934)	
	Conversion	−6.4402 (1.6570)**	0.0000
	1st year	−1.6537 (5.8281)	0.9639

Table D.4 (continued)

	Calculated with Student Fixed Effects OLS	p-value (charter + X)
2nd year	−1.3295 (2.9006)	0.8336
3rd year	−4.491 (3.0743)	0.3829

NOTES: There are no significant high school effects. All estimates include year and grade fixed effects. Standard errors are in parentheses.

*Significant at the 5 percent level.

**Significant at the 1 percent level.

Table D.5

Stanford 9 Test-Score Gain Regression Coefficients, Student Switching Behavior

		Calculated with Student Fixed Effects OLS Specification (No Conversion Control)	p-value (charter + X)	Calculated with Student Fixed Effects OLS Specification (Conversion Control)	p-value (charter + X)
Elementary School					
Math	Charter	−3.0976 (4.6123)		−4.6281 (5.2239)	
	Conversion			3.9633 (6.3512)	0.9124
	Switchercharter1	−6.8698 (3.7732)	0.0190	−6.5181 (3.8151)	0.0165
	Switchercharter2	2.1893 (3.0114)	0.8229	2.3367 (3.0207)	0.6202
	Switchernoncharter1	−1.2182 (0.6184)*		−1.2163 (0.6184)*	
	Switchernoncharter2	−0.2829 (0.5912)		−0.2709 (0.5915)	
Middle School					
Math	Charter	0.4388 (1.5347)		−3.1165 (2.1615)	
	Conversion			4.684 (2.0054)*	0.3300
	Switchercharter1	−0.329 (0.8204)	0.9426	−0.3842 (0.8207)	0.1069
	Switchercharter2	−0.6863 (1.2128)	0.8270	−0.8009 (1.2137)	0.0431
	Switchernoncharter1	−5.2124 (0.3150)**		−5.2334 (0.3151)**	
	Switchernoncharter2	−2.1316 (0.3970)**		−2.1193 (0.3970)**	
Reading	Charter	−1.8495 (1.5250)		2.357 (2.1347)	
	Conversion			−5.5714 (1.9786)**	0.0446
	Switchercharter1	−4.6756 (0.8173)**	0.0000	−4.6053 (0.8175)**	0.2941

172

Table D.5 (continued)

		Calculated with Student Fixed Effects OLS Specification (No Conversion Control)	p-value (charter + X)	Calculated with Student Fixed Effects OLS Specification (Conversion Control)	p-value (charter + X)
	Switchercharter2	0.446 (1.2055)	0.2113	0.5813 (1.2063)	0.1234
	Switchernoncharter1	−3.5393 (0.3116)**		−3.5144 (0.3117)**	
	Switchernoncharter2	−0.3409 (0.3922)		−0.3536 (0.3922)	
		High School			
Math	Charter	−1.5699 (2.0460)			
	Conversion				
	Switchercharter1	−0.9854 (1.6925)	0.2836		
	Switchercharter2	−0.6127 (2.2262)	0.2431		
	Switchernoncharter1	0.1904 (0.4600)			
	Switchernoncharter2	−1.2305 (0.5908)*			

NOTES: There are no significant elementary or high school reading effects. All estimates include year and grade fixed effects. Standard errors are in parentheses. There are no conversions at the high school level.

switchercharter1/switchernoncharter1: Student is at a different school than last year and the new school is a charter/noncharter.

switchercharter2/switchernoncharter2: Student is at a different school than two years ago and the new school is a charter/noncharter.

*Significant at the 5 percent level.

**Significant at the 1 percent level.

Table D.6

Estimated One-Year Effects of Switching to a Charter School, Measured in Proportion of Stanford 9 Test-Score Standard Deviation Units, by Race

			Elementary	Middle	High
Overall Charter Effect					
Hispanic	Math		−0.35	0.07	—
	Reading		—	−0.07	—
White	Math			—	−0.12
	Reading		—	—	—
Black	Math		—	—	—
	Reading		—	—	—
Asian	Math		—	−0.16	—
	Reading		—	—	—
Effect by Charter Type					
Hispanic	Math	Startup	−0.50	−0.13	—
		Conversion	—	0.10	—
	Reading	Startup	—	—	—
		Conversion	—	−0.08	—
White	Math	Startup	—	—	—
		Conversion	—	—	—
	Reading	Startup	—	—	—
		Conversion	—	—	—
Black	Math	Startup	—	0.16	—
		Conversion	—	—	—
	Reading	Startup	—	0.14	—
		Conversion	—	—	—
Asian	Math	Startup	—	—	—
		Conversion	−0.52	—	—
	Reading	Startup	—	—	—
		Conversion	—	—	—

NOTES: Blank entries indicate no statistically significant effects at the 5 percent level. The exception is the high school column, where separate estimates for conversion schools are not estimated because there are no conversions at the high school level.

Table D.7

Estimated Effects of Attending a Charter School on California Standards Test Score: Score Normalized to Mean 0, Standard Deviation 1, in Each Grade Span

	Fixed Effects OLS	Sample Sizes: Number of Students [Number of Observations]	Number of Charter Students	Anderson-Hsiao IV	Sample Sizes: Number of Students [Number of Observations]	Number of Charter Students
Elementary School						
Math	0.099 (0.0364)**	41,433 [59,393]	1,456	0.1025 (0.0375)**	17,960	599
Reading	−0.0364 (0.032)	40,375 [57,238]	1,384	−0.0228 (0.034)	16,863	546
Middle School						
Math	−0.1053 (0.0187)**	38,785 [55,626]	5,115	−0.068 (0.0145)**	25,540	3,266
Reading	−0.0413 (0.0155)**	38,130 [54,440]	4,962	−0.0588 (0.0124)**	24,714	3,125
High School						
Math	−0.0348 (0.027)	30,739 [43,285]	2,137	−0.0297 (0.020)	19,679	1,137
Reading	−0.0045 (0.021)	32,483 [45,571]	2,636	0.0132 (0.015)	20,008	1,264

NOTE: Standard errors are in parentheses.
*Significant at the 5 percent level.
**Significant at the 1 percent level.

Table D.8

Estimated Effects of Attending a Startup or Conversion Charter School on California Standards Test Score: Score Normalized to Mean 0, Standard Deviation 1, in Each Grade Span

		Student Fixed Effects OLS	Anderson Hsiao IV
Elementary School			
Math	Startup	0.1127 (0.0401)**	0.1154 (0.0414)**
	Conversion	0.0421 (0.0796)	0.0485 (0.0822)
Reading	Startup	−0.0581 (0.0352)	−0.0489 (0.0373)
	Conversion	0.0653 (0.0742)	0.1001 (0.0787)
Middle School			
Math	Startup	−0.2898 (0.0321)**	−0.2653 (0.0250)**
	Conversion	−0.0239 (0.0220)	0.0206 (0.0171)
Reading	Startup	−0.0343 (0.0262)	−0.0428 (0.0214)*
	Conversion	−0.0446 (0.0184)*	−0.066 (0.0147)**

NOTE: Standard errors are in parentheses.

*Significant at the 5 percent level.

**Significant at the 1 percent level.

References

Anderson, T. W., and Cheng Hsiao, "Formulation and Estimation of Dynamic Models Using Panel Data," *Journal of Econometrics*, Vol. 18, No. 1, January 1982, pp. 47–82.

Betts, Julian R., "Is There a Link Between School Inputs and Earnings? Fresh Scrutiny of an Old Literature," in Gary Burtless, ed., *Does Money Matter? The Effect of School Resources on Student Achievement and Adult Success*, Brookings Institution, Washington, D.C., 1996.

Betts, Julian R., and Anne Danenberg, "An Assessment of Resources and Student Achievement," in Jon Sonstelie and Peter Richardson, eds., *School Finance and California's Master Plan for Education*, Public Policy Institute of California, San Francisco, California, 2001, pp. 47–79.

Betts, Julian, Dan Goldhaber, and Larry Rosenstock, "The Supply Side of School Choice," Chapter 4 in Julian R. Betts and Tom Loveless, eds., *Getting Choice Right: Ensuring Equity and Efficiency in Education Policy*, Brookings Institution Press, Washington, D.C., 2005.

Betts, Julian R., Kim S. Rueben, and Anne Danenberg, *Equal Resources, Equal Outcomes? The Distribution of School Resources and Student Achievement in California*, Public Policy Institute of California, San Francisco, California, 2000.

Betts, Julian R., Andrew Zau, and Kevin King, *From Blueprint to Reality: San Diego's Education Reforms*, Public Policy Institute of California, San Francisco, California, 2005.

Betts, Julian R., Andrew Zau, and Lorien Rice, *Determinants of Student Achievement: New Evidence from San Diego*, Public Policy Institute of California, San Francisco, California, 2003.

Bifulco, Robert, and Helen F. Ladd, "The Impacts of Charter Schools on Student Achievement: Evidence from North Carolina," *Education Finance and Policy*, Vol. 1, No. 1, Winter 2006, pp. 50–90.

Black, Sandra E., "Do Better Schools Matter? Parental Valuation of Elementary Education," *Quarterly Journal of Economics*, Vol. 114, No. 2, May 1999, pp. 577–599.

Bloom, Howard S., "Sample Design for an Evaluation of the Reading First Program," MDRC Working Papers on Research Methodology, Manpower Demonstration Research Corporation, New York, 2003.

Coley, Richard J., *An Uneven Start: Indicators of Inequality in School Readiness*, Educational Testing Service, Princeton, New Jersey, 2002.

Cook, Thomas, David Armor, Robert Crain, Norman Miller, Walter Stephan, Herbert Walberg, and Paul Wortman, *School Desegregation and Black Achievement*, National Institute of Education, Washington, D.C., 1984.

Crain, Robert L., and Rita A. Mahard, "Minority Achievement: Policy Implications of Research," in Willis D. Hawley, ed., *Effective School Desegregation: Equity, Quality and Feasibility*, Sage Publications, Thousand Oaks, California, 1981.

Cullen, Julie Berry, Brian A. Jacob, and Steven Levitt, "The Effect of School Choice on Student Outcomes: Evidence from Randomized Lotteries," National Bureau of Economic Research, Working Paper 10113, Cambridge, Massachusetts, November 2003.

Cullen, Julie Berry, Brian Jacob, and Steven Levitt, "The Impact of School Choice on Student Outcomes: An Analysis of the Chicago Public Schools," National Bureau of Economic Research, Working Paper 7888, Cambridge, Massachusetts, September 2000.

Donner, Allan, and Neil Klar, *Design and Analysis of Cluster Randomization Trials in Health Research*, Arnold, London, and Oxford University Press, New York, 2000.

Fairlie, Robert W., and Alexandra M. Resch, "Is There 'White Flight' into Private Schools? Evidence from the National Educational Longitudinal Survey," *Review of Economics and Statistics*, Vol. 84, No. 1, February 2002, pp. 21–33.

Figlio, David, and Maurice Lucas, "What's in a Grade? School Report Cards and House Prices," *American Economic Review*, Vol. 88, No. 3, 2004, pp. 33–62.

Gill, Brian P., P. Michael Timpane, Karen E. Ross, and Dominic J. Brewer, *Rhetoric Versus Reality: What We Know and What We Need* to *Know About Vouchers and Charter Schools*, RAND Corporation, Santa Monica, California, 2001.

Hanushek, Eric A., "School Resources and Student Performance," in Gary Burtless, ed., *Does Money Matter? The Effect of School Resources on Student Achievement and Adult Success*, Brookings Institution, Washington, D.C., 1996, pp. 43–73.

Hanushek, Eric. A., John F. Kain, Steven G. Rivkin, and Gregory F. Branch, "Charter School Quality and Parental Decision Making with School Choice," National Bureau of Economic Research, Working Paper 11252, Cambridge, Massachusetts, March 2005.

Heckman, James, "Instrumental Variables: A Study of Implicit Behavioral Assumptions Used in Making Program Evaluations," *Journal of Human Resources*, Vol. 32, No. 3, Summer 1997, pp. 441–462.

Heckman, James J., Robert J. Lalonde, and Jeffrey A. Smith, "The Economics and Econometrics of Active Labor Market Programs," in Orley C. Ashenfelter and David Card, eds., *Handbook of Labor Economics, Volume 3*, 1999, pp. 1865–2097.

Howell, William G., and Paul E. Peterson, "The Education Gap: Vouchers and Urban Schools," Brookings Institution, Washington, D.C., 2002.

Hoxby, Caroline M., "Does Competition Among Public Schools Benefit Students and Taxpayers?" *American Economic Review*, Vol. 90, No. 5, 2000, pp. 1209–1238.

Jepsen, Christopher, and Steven Rivkin, *Class Size Reduction, Teacher Quality, and Academic Achievement in California Public Elementary Schools*, Public Policy Institute of California, San Francisco, California, 2002.

Krueger, Alan B., and Pei Zhu, "Another Look at the New York City School Voucher Experiment," National Bureau of Economic Research, Working Paper 9418, Cambridge, Massachusetts, January 2003.

Lukas, J. Anthony, *Common Ground: A Turbulent Decade in the Lives of Three American Families*, Knopf, New York, 1985.

Mahan, Aline M., and Thomas W. Mahan, "Changes in Cognitive Style: An Analysis of the Effect of White Suburban Schools on Inner City Children," *Integrated Education*, Vol. 8, No.1, 1970, pp. 58–61.

Mayer, Daniel P., Paul E. Peterson, David E. Myers, Christina Clark Tuttle, and William G. Howell, "School Choice in New York City After Three Years: An Evaluation of the School Choice Scholarships Program," Mathematica Policy Research, Inc., Washington, D.C., 2002.

McClure, Larry, Betsy Strick, Rachel Jacob-Almeida, and Christopher Reicher, "The Preuss School at UCSD: School Characteristics and Students' Achievement," The Center for Research on Educational Equity, Assessment and Teaching Effectiveness, UCSD, December 2005, available at http://create.ucsd.edu/Research_Evaluation/.

National Center for Education Statistics, "Common Core of Data," available at http://nces.ed.gov/ccd/ccddata.asp.

Raphael, Steven, and Lorien Rice, "Car Ownership, Employment, and Earnings," *Journal of Urban Economics*, Vol. 52, 2002, pp. 109–130.

Reback, Randall, "Supply and Demand in a Public School Choice Program," paper presented at the June Society of Labor Economists conference, Boston, Massachusetts, 2005.

Rice, Lorien, "Public Transit and Employment Outcomes," unpublished manuscript, University of California, San Diego, and Public Policy Institute of California, San Francisco, California, 2004.

Rothstein, Jesse, "Good Principals or Good Peers: Parental Valuation of School Characteristics, Tiebout Equilibrium, and the Incentive Effects of Competition Among Jurisdictions," National Bureau of Economic Research, Working Paper 10666, Cambridge, Massachusetts, August 2004.

Sass, Tim R., "Charter Schools and Student Achievement in Florida," *Education Finance and Policy*, Vol. 1, No. 1, Winter 2006, pp. 91–122.

Solmon, Lewis, Kern Paark, and David Garcia, *Does Charter School Attendance Improve Test Scores? The Arizona Results*, Goldwater Institute Center for Market-Based Education, Phoenix, Arizona, 2001.

Tiebout, Charles M., "A Pure Theory of Local Public Expenditures," *Journal of Political Economy*, Vol. 64, 1956, pp. 415–424.

Wooldridge, Jeffrey, "Cluster-Sample Methods in Applied Econometrics," *American Economic Review*, Vol. 93, No. 2, May 2003, pp. 133–138.

Zau, Andrew, and Julian Betts, "The Evolution of School Choice," in Frederick M. Hess, ed., *Urban School Reform: Lessons from San Diego,* Harvard Education Press, Cambridge, Massachusetts, 2005, pp. 223–241.

Zdep, Stanley M., "Educating Disadvantaged Urban Children in Suburban Schools: An Evaluation," *Journal of Applied Social Psychology*, Vol. 1, No. 2, 1971, pp. 173–186.

About the Authors

JULIAN R. BETTS

Julian Betts is a senior fellow at the Public Policy Institute of California and a professor of economics at the University of California, San Diego. Much of his research has focused on the economic analysis of public schools. He has written extensively on the link between student outcomes and measures of school spending, including class size and teacher qualifications. He has also studied the role that standards and expectations play in student achievement. He is serving or has served on numerous U.S. Department of Education technical review and grant adjudication committees, two National Research Council committees, The National Working Commission on Choice in K–12 Education, and the national advisory boards of both the Center for Research on Education Outcomes at Stanford University and the National Charter School Research Project at the University of Washington. He holds a Ph.D. in economics from Queen's University, Kingston, Ontario, Canada, and an M.Phil. in economics from Oxford University.

LORIEN A. RICE

Lorien Rice, an assistant professor of economics at Mills College, specializes in labor economics. Her research interests include poverty, transportation, education, and the distribution of income and wealth. Previously, she was a research fellow at PPIC, where her work focused on the role of transportation and geographic access in determining employment and educational outcomes. Earlier in her career, she worked at MDRC in New York, where she helped evaluate job training and education programs for disadvantaged populations. She also served as a socioeconomic planner for the Peace Corps in Morocco's National Park Service. She holds a B.A. in economics from Oberlin College and an M.A. and Ph.D. in economics from the University of California, San Diego.

ANDREW C. ZAU

Andrew Zau is a senior statistician in the Department of Economics at the University of California, San Diego. His current research focuses on the determinants of student achievement in the San Diego Unified School District. Before that, he was a research associate at PPIC, working on similar topics. He holds a B.S. in bioengineering from the University of California, San Diego, and an M.P.H. in epidemiology from San Diego State University.

Y. EMILY TANG

Y. Emily Tang is a Ph.D. candidate in the Department of Economics at the University of California, San Diego. She studies applied microeconomics and public finance. She has worked as a research assistant at the Brookings Institution and served as a summer fellow at Mathematica Policy Research, Inc. She holds a B.S. in economics and computer science from Duke University and an M.A. in economics from the University of California, San Diego.

CORY R. KOEDEL

Cory Koedel is a Ph.D. candidate in the Department of Economics at the University of California, San Diego. Most of his research has focused on the economic analysis of public schools, with an emphasis on teacher quality and school choice. In 2005, he received the Spencer Foundation's dissertation fellowship award. He holds a B.A. in economics and U.S. history and an M.A. in economics from the University of California, San Diego.

Related PPIC Publications

From Blueprint to Reality: San Diego's Education Reforms (2005)
Julian R. Betts, Andrew C. Zau, Kevin King

Determinants of Student Achievement: New Evidence from San Diego (2003)
Julian R. Betts, Andrew C. Zau, Lorien A. Rice

"An Assessment of Resources and Student Achievement," (2001)
Julian R. Betts and Anne Danenberg, in Jon Sonstelie and Peter Richardson, eds., *School Finance and California's Master Plan for Education*

Equal Resources, Equal Outcomes? The Distribution of School Resources and Student Achievement in California (2000)
Julian R. Betts, Kim S. Rueben, Anne Danenberg

PPIC publications may be ordered by phone or from our website
(800) 232-5343 [mainland U.S.]
(415) 291-4400 [outside mainland U.S.]
www.ppic.org